EVE NOAKES-OSBORNE

THE CHALK FACE

& BEYOND

Adventures in and out of the classroom

EVE NOAKES-OSBORNE

THE CHALK FACE & BEYOND

Adventures in and out of the classroom

MEREO
Cirencester

Mereo Books

1A The Wool Market Dyer Street Cirencester Gloucestershire GL7 2PR
An imprint of Memoirs Publishing www.mereobooks.com

The chalkface and beyond: 978-1-86151-220-8

First published in Great Britain in 2014
by Mereo Books, an imprint of Memoirs Publishing

Copyright ©2014

Eve Noakes-Osborne has asserted her right under the Copyright Designs and Patents
Act 1988 to be identified as the author of this work.

A CIP catalogue record for this book is available from the British Library.

The address for Memoirs Publishing Group Limited can be found at
www.memoirspublishing.com

The Memoirs Publishing Group Ltd Reg. No. 7834348

The Memoirs Publishing Group supports both The Forest Stewardship Council® (FSC®) and
the PEFC® leading international forest-certification organisations. Our books carrying both the
FSC label and the PEFC® and are printed on FSC®-certified paper. FSC® is the only
forest-certification scheme supported by the leading environmental organisations including
Greenpeace. Our paper procurement policy can be found at
www.memoirspublishing.com/environment

Cover design - Ray Lipscombe

Typeset in 11/16pt Bembo
by Wiltshire Associates Publisher Services Ltd. Printed and bound in Great Britain by
Printondemand-Worldwide, Peterborough PE2 6XD

FOREWORD

I grew up in the 1960s, the era of sex and drugs and rock and roll. When I began teaching in the 70s, I did not leave all that behind.

My story covers four decades of teaching in one primary school, but it is also a tale of a child of the 60s growing and experiencing life and the changes which I encountered in my professional and private life culminating in my retirement.

DEDICATION

My book is dedicated to the children, colleagues and friends I have met along the way, many of whom are mentioned and many of whom are not, but the vast majority of whom are fondly remembered.

Chapter 1

I began a long teaching career in 1974 at the age of 23. The appearance of the school where I began my career appealed to me. It was a modern building which resembled a high school rather than the middle school it was. I retained a desire to teach older children, but I had been thrown out of teachers' training college with a comment from the Principal, 'And what makes you think you should ever teach older children? You can hardly control your own life, let alone control teenagers!'

Only on the proviso that I should teach at primary level was I eventually allowed to continue and finish my course.

After my demeaning expulsion from college (I was burning the candle at both ends, taking illicit drugs and experimenting with life) I became a student teacher for two terms. Then I was reassessed and finished my course. I had always loved the teaching practices – I was just hopeless at the boring essay writing. I copied most of my essays from friends for my finals and fabricated my dissertation, which was based on 100 responses to a questionnaire about truancy. I made up the results but I passed. I never picked up my certificate, but the DFES assures me I am indeed a qualified teacher, which is a relief after 37 years in the job!

So here I was on the eve of the first day of term, meeting my new colleagues, four of whom were 'probationers', like me. I don't think any of us really knew what was in store for us. I was to have a second-year class of 39 8-9 year olds. The school took pupils up to the age of 12 and had a roll of 423 in the Middle School. The First School was on the same site with a different head and we had very little interaction between the two schools. The heads were like chalk and cheese.

My first head teacher, Mr John Thomas, was not adverse to humiliating young staff in front of 400 pupils in the school hall or, indeed, battering badly-behaved pupils during assembly. He spent most afternoons asleep in his room. His secretary, Janet Parkyns, was similar to a doctors' receptionist. 'What's the matter? Why do you want to speak to him?' she would say. Unless someone was dying, she refused to disturb him.

As I sat down in the staff room on that first day I was able to survey my fellow teachers. Some were very aged. Mr Thomas, 'Tommy', was well into his fifties and was one of the 'old school'. Modern teaching styles and methods had passed him by. He wore the same old shapeless suit every day. He was generally a miserable old bugger but a good funeral, or a visit to the dentist, always cheered him up. Tommy was very much a 'spare the rod and spoil the child' advocate. In those days corporal punishment had not yet been banned, so Tommy always kept the cane well-oiled and used it quite often.

Miss Hilda Yeoman, his deputy, was an old spinster with a great personality whom I grew to admire and like immensely. She would sit smoking her fags in the staffroom with her legs open and her bloomers on display. The ash would grow longer and longer on the end of her cigarette until it fell off in a heap on the carpet beneath her. Hilda was a harridan, a scary disciplinarian as far as the children were concerned but a lady who had a droll, sarcastic wit and whom I liked enormously. I never did understand her domestic arrangements. She lived with a female friend and I wondered if she was in a lesbian relationship (unheard of in those days), but I never found out.

Of the probationers there was Penny, an innocent: very pure and naive. As time went on Tommy began to give her a hard time. She was a good teacher, much liked by the children, but she wasn't able to stand up to Tommy's bullying. Oh yes, he was often worse with the teachers than he was with the children. One day, during our first year, he had been so cruel that he had made Penny cry. On receipt of a phone call, Tommy immediately went back into her classroom and apologised. He had found out that her father was a mason, as he himself was. He left her alone after that. The old boy network!

Pam, another probationer, was a very beautiful natural redhead. She taught home economics. Although only 21 and in her first post, she was already married. Not surprisingly her husband, a milkman, had snapped her up. He was a nice guy and their relationship was solid. Pam was a lovely person. She didn't stay long at our school but moved out to the countryside after a couple of years. Strangely, I remember that she had never grown any adult teeth (odd how you remember things like that!)

Pam didn't really socialise with the rest of us at the disco evenings held at the teachers' centre on Friday nights. After all, we (the young female teachers) went to try to hook up with the young male teachers. She had no need to, but she did forge a strong bond with Anne-Marie, another probationer. Anne-Marie was a twin. She had a very pretty sister who had the looks while Anne-Marie had a slight turn in her eye, and I think she must have found it difficult when compared to her twin. But she had a strong personality, was great fun and, I heard, went on to climb the teaching ladder. I wonder if, like me, they are retired now.

The other probationer was Diane, who was also married; same age as us. One amusing anecdote from Diane was when a naughty boy in her class, trying to gain her attention, shouted across the classroom, 'Oi, you, I'm talking to you!' We all had a good laugh about that, including Diane.

Her marriage seemed strong and we were all stunned to be told that later, when she and her husband had moved out of London, that she had found her husband *in flagrante* with a colleague of his.

And then of course there was me.

I'm a fairly strong, confident character. When starting teaching I'd coped with a series of failed relationships with no ill effect. I always seemed to be able to bounce back. I'd loved drama and had appeared in many amateur plays, and teaching is a great path for would-be actors. The classroom is a stage where you can bring life to every aspect of your teaching and where, as long as you *are* acting, you can show a range of feelings to create the response you want from the pupils. The danger only comes when the anger is real.

There were many other key members of staff, many of whom had a specialism. Middle schools taught children specific lessons such as Design Technology, Cookery, French, Science and Needlework. As a result I had eight free periods per week - bliss.

I had an evening job at a pub! There was no planning for lessons. You chose what interested you, closed your classroom door and no one questioned what you were doing. The children became caught up in your enthusiasm and we were never bored.

Chapter 2

—————✗—————

The school stood, and indeed stands to this day, in its own grounds, which were, and remain, expansive; the largest in the borough for a primary school, as it now is. Mind you, there was an apprehensive moment when a group of Sikh gentlemen prowled the grounds with a view to buy! I think their intention might have been to build a gurdwara (a Sikh temple) on our prime site. This was a long time ago. I am delighted to say that the local council managed to retain control of the site, and it remains a primary school. Well -established trees and flowerbeds created a feeling of being out in the countryside, while in fact it lay in an urban environment.

The surrounding roads were a middle-class enclave. As you approached the school, you viewed well-kept detached and semi-detached houses with pretty gardens. Little could anyone know at the time, least of all me, that the school was to become a recipient of the newly-arriving influx of peoples from Asia and Uganda. Thus I was surprised when viewing the playground on my first day of teaching to see coachloads of children who had been bussed from the centre of Southall to our school in the 'leafy suburbs'. Central Southall couldn't cope with the number of new immigrants and therefore the surrounding schools had to take the overflow.

With my nerves on edge – my first class, my first year - I hadn't slept well the night before. In 36 years of new beginnings this feeling of apprehension, fear and doubt always remained at the beginning of each year; it was something I never conquered.

I had prepared as well as I could the previous day by placing the desks where I thought they should be and collecting the exercise books for the children. Although the classrooms were a reasonable size, with 39 children it meant that once they were seated there was no chance of them moving, or indeed of me moving amongst them. The desks were old-fashioned ones which opened at the top. This meant that uneaten packed lunches and smelly PE kits often festered inside them.

I brought the children into the classroom, they sat down and I began to call the register. Obviously I had no problems with the Davids and Pauls, but Pratpinderpal and Rajwant were a little more challenging, especially since I was completely confused as to whether they were girls or boys. The vast majority of the children with unfamiliar names seemed to have plaits, many of them worn on the tops of their heads. I discovered later that these were Sikh boys. Initially I assumed they were all girls. It didn't take me too long to discover that I didn't have quite as many girls as I thought!

At the end of the school year we had to fill in report cards for the children, blue for a boy and pink for a girl. One of the male teachers, Bill Kirkpatrick, an interesting character in his fifties who taught music while also having his own class, completed a pink card for a boy who had been in his class all year, referring to 'her' many abilities and shortcomings! I'll tell you more about Bill later.

Taripatraj Rhandowa was a particular name I loved and have never forgotten. She was a Tamil girl in my first class from Sri Lanka and she was lovely. The unfamiliar names and customs of the children took me some time to understand. If I thought back I couldn't honestly remember the ethnic make-up of that first class or any other until the end of my teaching. I would have to make a conscious effort to think about how many white, Asian, West Indian, Somalian etc children I have had in my classes. It becomes totally unimportant and irrelevant. It has always been the individual child that mattered most.

However, the overflow into the school of children from ethnic backgrounds had an impact. There were quite a few children of white English origin. The school, as I have said, was in a prime location - on the surface. Some children came from middle-class families who lived on the nearby estate. I am referring to expensive properties in the immediate catchment areas. Many children of our school age were increasingly being transferred to private fee-paying schools, their parents objecting to the change of intake.

The school is alongside the Grand Union Canal. The side on which the school was situated was affluent. On the other side of the canal was the Havelock Estate, built in the early 1950s as a council estate. Many of our white intake came from troubled backgrounds on this estate and brought their problems to school with them. Their home lives were difficult. There was little income, and theft and drug-taking were commonplace on the estate in the 70s and 80s. Some of these children were pupils in my class.

The children of the newly-arrived families were generally extremely hard-working and well behaved. Their parents, having been given a new chance of a better life, supported us, as teachers, in every way. They listened with respect, encouraged their children and were making the very best of their new opportunities. We had an assessment centre on site. This was where children with no spoken English were taught the basics so that they could integrate into the school system. We did have a problem with names and indeed dates of birth of new arrivals. The births had often not been registered and a lot of the boys arrived with the last name of Singh – merely denoting a lion or male in Hinduism or Sikhism - and Kaur (princess) for the girls.

Gian Singh was in my first class. He was new to England and new to English. At that time in school it was the policy not to allow pupils to speak in their own language in either the classroom or the playground. Were we perhaps threatened by what they might be saying? Poor Gian had to cope entirely alone to understand this new world he had entered. At least in this respect things have improved today. Children new to English are now paired, where possible, with other students or adults who have the same native language to help them make sense of the new world they have found themselves in.

And so my first class was a mishmash of cultures. I did have a smattering of children of West Indian or mixed race. Andrea George gave me some grief! She was a dominant girl of West Indian background who had a little entourage of admirers. She took an instant dislike to me. I would notice her glaring at me whenever I gave any instructions and it took a while before we built up any sort of relationship. But we managed it in the end.

Chapter 3

I don't have a clue what I taught during that first week. What I do remember is that it was hard, very hard. Not the teaching but the discipline. Imagine standing in front of 39 little individuals trying to teach and engage them when they have a completely different agenda from you; school is for socialising, chatting to your friends. My dad, now deceased, thought that teaching was a doddle. Short hours, long holidays. How hard could it be? He was a bigwig in ICI. He had no idea, and many people still don't know how intimidating a bunch of kids can be.

As I recall, school began on a Tuesday. By the following Tuesday I was at my wits' end. They didn't listen. They didn't do what I told them to, and they weren't very nice.

My brother Ken, six years older, with a degree in Geography from Reading University, had decided to teach in a primary school. He had the advantage over me. He had already been teaching for four years, was a man (much easier in terms of discipline since male primary school teachers were rare and were generally held in great respect.) He was doing very well, thank you. No problems. I vividly remember driving from my school to his one day after school asking him what I should do about my total inability to tame these children. The one piece of advice he gave me, which has stayed with me forever, was, 'All you have to remember is that it's either them or you!' It made the world of difference. I had to make sure I won the battle, and in the end I did.

Of course all of us probationers were finding things a little tricky and we sympathised, commiserated and laughed together about the situation we found ourselves in. Many of the established staff were very supportive. Just mention anything to Miss Yeoman and she was on the case. Mr Vizard, the Science teacher, who was in his forties, was truly wonderful. A gentle, charming and wonderfully calm man, he was always ready to support and help us. He apparently had an extremely neurotic, demanding wife whom I never met. How he managed to be so wonderful every day when he had a world of anxiety at home I don't know. Although that isn't entirely true. During my life in teaching there have been times when being at school, where you are able to forget your 'other life', can bring a sort of sanity.

I often think I was saved in that first term by the arrival of a student teacher. Goodness! How was I supposed to help a student when I had no experience myself? But such was the teaching system in 1974. I can't remember her name but she was in her final year of teacher training, which meant she would virtually take over my class. This had a wonderful effect on my pupils. They then viewed me as their real teacher, and my status with them increased enormously.

It was great for me. Not only did I have the eight free periods, but for the rest of the time I just took small groups of children in the corridor to help them in different lessons. This allowed me to build up my relationships with the children and we began to mould as a class.

Having said that, there was an occasion in those early days when having such a large class had certain problems. I don't remember the details, but David, a little ginger-haired boy, was admonished by me for something he must have done. No idea what! The next thing I knew was Mr Thomas entering my classroom and asking where he was. I looked around and realised he wasn't there. Tommy said 'No, that's because his mother has just phoned the school to say he's at home.' I hadn't even missed him. Thank goodness for electronic gates and CCTV cameras!

Tommy didn't make a big deal about David, the runaway. But he did make a big deal of most other things. In those days we had a Banda machine – no photocopiers. The Banda machine involved making a carbon copy which you attached to the machine, turning the handle to make multiple copies. David became extremely annoyed with Kathy Barratt, the Maths teacher, because she had used the Banda to make 40 copies of a clock face so that each member of her Maths group could use them to show different times. A complete waste of resources, he claimed!

But Tommy had a heat copier. This, I think, made one copy of a page of a book (I don't think anyone worried about copyright), which would then make endless copies. It was new and he wouldn't allow anyone but himself to use it. It went wrong almost every time he tried, but it was his baby. You would ask him if he could make a copy and he would happily spend hours attempting to. He'd eventually emerge triumphant with ink all over his hands. He never missed his afternoon nap, though.

Our staff meetings were interesting. I don't recall them ever focusing on anything to do with teaching. They usually revolved around the excess use of resources – paper, books, pencils etc. As probationers we didn't really have any say in anything. We were young, so we would tend to sit quietly and listen to what Tommy had to say while thinking individually how irascible he was.

Tommy's assemblies were legend. The children would file into the hall in rows, the older children toward the back of the hall. There were a lot of children and there was very little room. The staff sat closest to their classes on either side of the hall. I was always furthest away from the hall doors. In that first year I was terrified of the oldest children. I was never sure, if I told them off for talking, whether they would respond or completely ignore me.

Tommy saw himself as a violinist, so the violin was often a part of the assembly, usually at the end. It was a painful experience (he didn't play well) but of course everyone pretended to sit in awe and wonder. We would make sure the children were seated by ten past nine. This was a great way to start the day. The assemblies often didn't finish until 10.00!

Tommy would use these assemblies to tell stories and facts gleaned from listening to Radio 4 that morning. Much of what he imparted was completely irrelevant or above their heads. I was astonished when he told the Asian pupils that if Hitler had won the war they would either have not been here or would have been used for his experiments. His favourite song was 'St Patrick's Breast Plate' and every day we prayed to a Christian God and every day we said the Lord's Prayer. The idea was that Mr Thomas would say one line and the children would repeat what he had said. One day Tommy began 'Our Father who art in Heaven' and the children responded 'Our Father who art in Heaven', but somewhere along the way things went wrong. By the end 400 children were saying the words and Tommy was giving the response! When he eventually realised what was happening he went ballistic. As staff, we thought it was hilarious but we didn't dare laugh out loud.

Sonny Neill Parker may well have prayed to his god, as he was brought on stage during one assembly. Tommy described to all assembled Sonny's misdemeanours. For the life of me I don't know what they were. All I remember is him asking if the child was sorry for what he had done. Probably because he was so scared, the boy did not reply. Mr Thomas then beat him physically with his hands several times in front of the assembled children and staff. I recall being totally disgusted. However, as I have said, I sat on the far side of the hall and I was frightened that if I had attempted to leave the hall he would have said, 'And where do you think you are going, Miss Noakes?' I don't think I have ever been so appalled by anything so close at hand in my whole life.

No one was safe when Mr Thomas was around. I've mentioned the fact that resources at school appeared to be more important than teaching, but hey, who was I? Maybe budgets in those days were the most important part of a head teacher's life. During one assembly in those early days he told Anne Marie, 'And you, Miss Hillier, have had 193 pencils so far this term!' The statement was meant to humiliate the teacher, not the class, and it did.

There were, of course, naughty kids. One of Tommy's

methods of understanding and supporting them was inviting them to his violin classes on a Friday afternoon. They were released from lessons and he 'taught' them how to play the violin. Not once did they give a recitation, and not once did we, as teachers, see any signs of interest amongst these children. In truth it was a cop out. No lessons, let's amuse Mr Thomas. Equally Miss Perry, the head of the first school, used to have a club for naughty boys where they were given sweets. The same children seemed to progress from one to another as they became older. We didn't mind. At least it was a calm end to the week.

Chapter 4

As I've intimated, teaching in the 70s was very different. For a start there was no written planning and no accountability. The only tests the children had were ones which we as teachers set and marked, really to measure that the pupils had learnt and remembered what we had taught them during the year. It was more to keep a check on our own success as teachers than anything else. There was no curriculum as such. We had outdated text books in English and Maths for each year group and we used these to gauge what we should teach.

English teaching tended to concentrate on imparting the rules of grammar and punctuation. This became very unfashionable later – 'just let them write' was the new philosophy. It was never an approach I agreed with. As with many initiatives in teaching, things have now come full circle. Children need the tools to succeed. They do not all learn by osmosis.

There was no setting for either Maths or English, so teaching 39 children of different abilities was challenging. We did have remedial withdrawal groups which supported those with the greatest needs. Differentiation followed the main teaching part of the lessons and the children tended to work through graduated exercises. There was little practical work (this would have been very difficult with such large classes) and little 'Talk for Writing' (a methodology which encouraged the children to discuss their ideas verbally, dramatically or in picture form before they put pencil to paper) so things have improved since then. I did use a lot of drama activities, probably far more than in recent years. We had more time. The kids loved it and there was no marking!

Marking, however, wasn't a problem. With four hours a week out of the classroom, all the children's work was marked during the day. Therefore it was easy to have an evening job in a pub every night of the week, as I did.

Having said this, I would spend all day Sunday planning activities to support teaching in History and Geography. We had carte blanche to teach themes that interested us. Native American Indians, Aborigines, Ancient China, Aztecs and Incas were just some examples. Days would be spent turning the classroom into a Red Indian village or a Chinese town. Literacy and numeracy lessons would reinforce the field of study. We'd dress up, sing, dance and create pictures and models. We cooked food, learnt games and even tried learning a few words in a different language. It was amazing fun for me and the children.

We'd share our knowledge with children in other classes. A day a term would be put aside so that each class could entertain and 'visit' other parts of the world. The children would work in groups, displaying their own work on pinboards in the classroom. They'd decide how they would present what they had learnt to other classes. They'd make and 'sell' artefacts to each other. It was a great experience, and one in which the children became animated and grew in confidence.

We had no Sats tests to work towards. There were no levels for the children to achieve and yet they enjoyed school and looked forward to the next project. There wasn't a sense of failure, as there is today when a child's inability to reach certain levels of attainment is reinforced time and time again from the endless testing. Many children returned to visit us, proud of the success they had made of their lives, of their place at university and their fond memories of the education they had received while they were with us.

Open evenings were a way in which the parents could see the results of all our hard work, and they were very appreciative. Many of the parents had newly arrived and spoke little English. The mums tended to be the ones who turned up with a posse of little people following them. We had staff who were able to translate, or the families would help each other out, with one mum translating for another. Whether native English speakers or not, the parents generally listened and responded to what we told them. Open evenings in those days were open events. There was no privacy. Parents entered the classroom and we as teachers spoke to them as best we could, in hushed voices, hoping that other parents would be unable to hear. It didn't always work. Mr Mahmoud said of another child, 'And I quite agree with you Miss Noakes. Their boy is an absolute nightmare'. Today we have private appointments, thank goodness.

I clearly remember one open evening when, while discussing the progress of a child, I saw a family of mice running around the back of the classroom. I mentioned this to the dad, who didn't bat an eyelid but simply continued talking about his son.

I put my feet up on a chair and attempted to carry on. I told the caretaker the next day! But I did have conversations later with the children in which it became obvious that vermin in their houses was not an unusual event.

We received few challenging questions. On the whole the parents were not sufficiently knowledgeable about the education system in this country to put us on the spot, as I am sure they were in more affluent areas. They accepted most comments that were made to them and usually kept their children in order. Many had been given this amazing opportunity of living in a new country and they valued and appreciated that.

Of course this didn't apply to our entire intake and it was often the families of lower working-class origin who gave us the most problems. It was either never their child's fault or the family was so dysfunctional that the parent (many single mums) or parents were totally unable to control their children.

We had a family of West Indian children, the Josephs. I think there was only a mum. I never met or heard of a dad being on the scene. The eldest boy, Dwayne, was OK; small in stature, not terribly bright, but nice enough.

Dwayne had two younger brothers, Winston and Errol, and they were a nightmare. There was nine months between them! They had been in Miss Perry's special club in the First School and Mr Thomas' violin club when they reached Middle School. We used to sell raffle tickets for summer fairs and the like. The boys made a reasonable living selling them to the elderly in the neighbourhood and pocketing the profits.

They saw a new opportunity when the mosque opened. They would nip in and steal the shoes and sell them on to a fence. Things became a little more serious when they were found breaking into school attempting to steal the old BBC computers. Right little entrepreneurs!

And of course they were naughty in lessons. I never taught either of them, but colleagues who did had a tough time. Interestingly and sadly, I met Winston not so long ago outside my local Tesco. He was charming and remembered me. His brother had been shot dead a couple of years earlier!

Jonny Denton was the bane of my life. He was an intelligent, good-looking boy who was an excellent sportsman. He absolutely adored football. Jonny was dreadful with me - very challenging, rude, badly behaved and extremely difficult. He had an older sister, Tracy, who had a mind of her own but who generally toed the line, and two younger brothers, Joel and Gary. At one point I was at my wits' end and spoke to Mr Thomas about him. Tommy called him into his office. The next thing I knew Mr Thomas was chasing Jonny down the school corridor shouting, 'Come back here boy, I'm going to cane you'.

Jonny was home before Tommy got to the bottom of the stairs. Mum duly brought him back and we spoke. I told her the situation from my point of view and said that the only punishment I could think of working was to stop him playing football. She replied, 'I don't think that will work. It will only make him worse. You're asking for trouble!' There was little support. Anyway I carried out my threat. He was spared the rod and guess what - it worked. I taught Jonny the following year as well and we had an understanding. When I left after my first three years he gave me a kiss on the cheek.

We were under a Labour government. I voted Labour. I

believed that we should help those families who couldn't help themselves. It became apparent as time went on that there were some people who expected help without deserving it. I was teaching some children whose families gave nothing but expected everything. They knew how to play the system. But this did not, by any means, apply to all of our families. Many sincerely wanted their children to do well.

Chapter 5

Anyway, we all got through our first year, despite Mr Thomas. We had one visit from someone important from the borough who glanced through our teaching files, which were flimsy at best, but I think we were all doing what mattered, which was teaching the children well and with enthusiasm. We had all passed our probationary year. We had established ourselves and were beginning to understand and respond to the children in our care.

Now it was time to make a difference. We all had interests which were outside the normal school hours. No, I'm not talking about our private lives. Everyone ran out-of-hours clubs. There were netball teams, often playing against other schools, football, athletics, hockey, science, cookery. You name it, we did it. We didn't expect to be paid. We didn't want thanks. We did it for the children.

No curriculum meetings, no team meetings, no planning meetings. Our time when the school day was over was our own. Sometimes if there were no clubs to run we would slope off to the staffroom and hardly move again until we were thrown off site by the caretaker at six o'clock. It was chill-out time. Very often there was a box of wine. We'd sit, sup and relax. We'd get to know each other. Talk about our private lives and laugh about the events of the day. It built a bond between the staff, a bond that meant we faced the children and the struggles of teaching together.

The school day was different from today. School started at 8.55, as today, and morning playtime was 10.40. It became a bit of a contest amongst the staff as to who could extend playtime the longest. There were over 400 children in the playground with two teachers. I don't recall fights and any arguments were easily sorted. Maybe with so many children they had little room in which to move around or make mischief. There were hardly any footballs, although of course the boys tended to dominate the middle of the playground.

We also had a much longer lunchtime, 12 noon until 1.25, and there was an afternoon playtime of 20 minutes. School finished at 3.40.

What with Mr Thomas' endless assemblies, lengthy playtimes and free periods, we actually spent little time in the classroom, but when we did it was quality time. In those days we used a whistle at the end of playtime. One blow meant stand still and then we would call out a year group. The children would then file into school, one year after another. I honestly don't recall that being a problem. Today classes line up in ranks endlessly waiting for the previous year group to go into school. Teachers now drill the children so that they enter school in 'silence'. It can take ten minutes until every child is in class ready and settled for the start of the day. I'm not sure the current system is better. It takes responsibility away from the children and expects unnatural behaviour from them. What's wrong with a chat with friends?

If a child was late arriving at school in the morning they had to contend with Mrs Parkyns, the short-tempered school secretary. She gave the children and their parents hell. Janet Parkyns was very protective of Tommy and very intolerant of us, the new teachers. Difficult to approach, she seemed to work to her own agenda. It gave her power, perhaps the power which was lacking in her home life. I never met her family. Her husband worked for EMI and she was fiercely protective of his job. She hated the new technology whereby you could access a range of resources without paying for them, because it meant that his job was in jeopardy. She had a daughter who moved to Rhodesia. She clearly loved her, but there was a difficulty about their relationship which she hinted at but never clearly explained.

It was strange how my relationship with her changed. On being told she wouldn't do what I asked (I really don't remember the facts – it was probably trivial) I reacted. I stood up to her. I refused to accept what she told me. Oddly, I immediately rose enormously in her estimation. I could do no wrong. I always showed respect to her and was polite, but she was a changed woman. She suddenly joined us in the staffroom after school, chatted, opened up and I think enjoyed her time with us. We began to see the soft, vulnerable side of Janet.

Unfortunately Janet's husband was suddenly admitted to Ealing hospital. They were both smokers. So am I, so I don't judge. He had his leg amputated and things went from worse to worse. I won't bore you with the gory details, but he died in hospital. Janet retired and moved to be with her daughter in Rhodesia and sadly we found out that within six months she also passed away. But it had been good for me and her that before she left she had at least, possibly for the first time in her life, opened up to someone. Those after-school relaxation times had proved very important to her!

Chapter 6

⚯

So year 2 began. Hey, so now I was an experienced, qualified teacher? No way! In teaching there is always so much to learn. A new class, same age range, roughly the same number of children. I did not only have a very large number of children to contend with; I also had two children with specific physical and mental disabilities.

Joanne had a mild form of Down's syndrome. She was a sweet little girl who was gentle and willing. Academically, Joanne needed help with her learning but she tried hard and seemed happy. She had many supportive girl friends and coped well with mainstream school.

David was fabulous. He had been born without joints in his knees and elbows. An intelligent boy, he was, academically, well able to cope with all main stream subjects. He was very popular with his classmates, who I am sure admired him while simply accepting the fact that he was different. They had known him since he had begun school.

David swung his legs from side to side when moving from place to place. This was the only way he was able to get around. We had stairs down into the playground which of course created difficulties, but not for David. He took it in his stride - sorry for the pun. Wow, he was a real character. He was extremely well behaved and loved by his peers, and his handwriting, considering the fact that he was unable to bend his arms, was possibly among the best in the classroom. David was a bright boy. His ambition was to become a pilot. Many years later he returned to school and we raised money for him so that he could have a car adapted to his needs. I don't think he was able to fulfil his ambition, but he had developed into a lovely young man.

Later, Matthew became a member of another of my classes. He was also a lovely boy. He had been born with no sexual organs. His parents had to make a decision at birth to select his gender. He was the first born, and later his parents had a son. In Matthew's case his parents decided they wanted him to become a boy. He had many operations to make this possible. By the time he was in my class, he was about eight years old and it seemed to me that perhaps they had made the wrong decision. Matthew was a gentle child. He was slightly effeminate, if you can say that of a boy at such a young age. He related better to the girls and disliked the rough, tough world of the boys. He later went on to become a teacher in a primary school, where I hope he was accepted and where I am sure he gave a valued contribution.

We also had children who had experienced horrific situations in their lives. There was Kajal, a little Pakistani girl, who had been made to sleep in a garden shed in her new English home. She wasn't wanted. She was a girl, not a boy, and as such would provide nothing for her family. Her predicament only came to light when concerned neighbours informed social services. At school I am sorry to say we were unaware. Although dirty, always wearing the same clothes (no uniforms in those days), she presented as a fairly 'normal' child, if somewhat shy and timid and in need of support academically.

There was the Davis family, Roger, Peter and Mandy. Mum was an alcoholic. Guy, the dad, was unkempt but he actually did care about his kids and would come to school whenever needed. Roger, the eldest son, was an intense, closed, intelligent boy who never spoke or complained about his home life. Peter was gorgeous, also intelligent. He certainly had a way with words. He once said to me when he was nine, 'You are the sugar in my tea'. It may not sound amazing in retrospect but it was eloquent and meant a great deal to me at the time. When the nursery staff went round for a home visit as Mandy was about to start school, they found rats running through the house and dog excrement in every room.

But I am sure each school has its own share of children with disabilities or endlessly sad situations. Sometimes I walk the streets and wonder where those children are, the children with Down's syndrome, those confined to wheelchairs, the children with physical or mental disabilities. By accepting them as part of our community we learn to understand and accept that not everyone is born perfect. When I was little I saw many people in the community, in the shops, in the streets, in the park, who clearly had something wrong with them. I didn't understand, I was a little frightened but my mum helped me to empathise and accept. Today these sights are hidden from us. The people are collected from their homes, delivered to a care centre and transported back home again. Yes, you could say this is the best way to care for people in the community, but it also means that when we see them we don't know how to react. Do we look away or laugh, as many children do, because they don't understand? The Paralympics are fantastic, but it is a special 'stage'. It isn't really part of everyday life and maybe children need to learn that it's OK to be different.

In our second year of teaching, we were all up for new challenges. Anne Marie was sporty, and following the enthusiasm for Olga Korbut and the Olympics, Ealing had established a gym competition for primary-school children. As a result she began an after-school gym club for our kids and I helped and learned from her. My understanding and enthusiasm continued long after she left. The gymnastic clubs became a huge part of my life and the life of the school.

Teachers new to our school arrived. Bill Kirkpatrick, who I have mentioned before, was one. Bill had a past entrenched in Tin Pan Alley. His background revolved around music and he came to us not only as a class teacher but also as a music specialist. Although he was in his fifties, I built a companionship with him. I found his knowledge of music fascinating and was impressed by his experience. I viewed Bill as a friend. We used to slope off at lunchtime to eat at lovely restaurants in Ealing, often arriving back to school late and just slightly inebriated. Amazingly our classes, next to each other in hutted accommodation, just waited patiently for us. Imagine that today, waiting patiently, chatting to each other! There was an occasion when members of my class told Mr Vizard that they could smell alcohol on my breath after lunch. He kindly told me to be wary, but denied to the children that this could be possible. What a lovely man!

My relationship with Bill was one in which I enjoyed his company and his experience of life. I was 24 and he was much, much older. He was divorced and lived on his own in Greenford. He asked me to dinner one evening, when it became clear that he wanted more than just friendship. In no way was I attracted to him physically – just the reverse. It was sad when I had to explain that this was not what I wanted. At school our friendship was mostly unaffected, but we didn't pop off for lunch anymore!

Miss Yeoman retired and a new, much younger, deputy head joined us. Jeff was someone I always felt endlessly sad about. Here he was with his first deputy headship, lots of great ideas and a really nice guy. But then there was Mr Thomas to contend with. Bless him, Jeff tried his best to support us and he tried to change things for the better. We were a school stuck in a void because we had a head teacher who was far too set in his ways. For goodness sake we had to account for every resource we used, we had huge classes with no help, and we had no structure, outdated textbooks and outdated teaching resources.

Jeff wanted to change things. He didn't succeed. There were many occasions, usually during staff meetings when he tried to challenge some of Tommy's decisions. If we had been older, more confident, perhaps less afraid of Tommy picking on us, we might have supported Jeff better. However, he was often loudly and humiliatingly put down.

Chapter 7

⸻※⸻

At the end of my second year of teaching, I was given the opportunity to go on the school journey. Anne Marie and I were to take a group of the oldest children on a camping holiday to Henley. Not far from where we taught, a short journey. How difficult could that be?

Henley, as probably everyone knows, is a pleasant middle-class enclave to the north-east of London. People went to expensive restaurants in Henley. Properties were worth millions then and even more now. So here we were taking a group of perhaps not-so-privileged kids from Southall to Henley. This was my first and last school journey.

We were booked into a Scout camp beside the river Thames. How lovely! We had lots of activities arranged for the children, all very organised. Canoeing, swimming, many water-related activities.

The short journey there was fine, simplicity itself. I wasn't familiar with the children, but they seemed a nice enough bunch. Anne Marie taught the same year group, so knew them better.

We arrived and the first task was to erect the tents. There

were no built-in fly sheets, which naturally meant that bugs could easily get inside, but what the heck. We were here to have an experience. Somehow or other we managed to put up the tents and sort out the sleeping bags.

Kids being kids, food was required. We set up camping stoves and started to cook sausages and baked beans and there was bread and margarine to fill them up. When we delivered the food, which smelt delicious, as camp food often does, Jonathon Simpson, a precious, spoilt little soul, announced loudly 'I don't eat margarine. I only have butter at home'. Our response was polite but to the point: 'Eat it or go without'.

The site was used by many schools. There were lots of groups of children from all over London, most of them teenagers and, as it happened, all except for our party were boys! So the girls we had with us created a lot of interest. Some of them were 12 going on 16.

After the evening meal we attempted a campfire singing session, but it began to rain; to rain heavily. The tents became soaked and water seeped inside. The site organiser came to us and suggested that the girls could move into a block of rooms which were well protected. This was in the days before equality. We roused the girls and moved them into the pleasant, cosy rooms. The boys, and indeed the two of us, just had to stick it out.

By now it was about 10 o'clock and I was knackered. All I wanted to do was go to sleep. Hah! Once we'd managed to sort out the girls, we went back to our tent.

Suddenly we noticed flashlights outside the girls' block.

'Come on, something's happening,' Anne Marie said.

'Oh god, what?' I replied. We put our coats over our pyjamas and crept over to the girls' block. Most of them were running around in their pyjamas, the lights were on and there was a bunch of teenage boys outside, enjoying the spectacle. Screams issued from one of the rooms as we entered and two little Asian girls were crying hysterically.

'Miss Hillier, they're looking at us. My dad'll kill me,' sobbed Kamaljit.

'Send them away, Miss Noakes!' her friend Ruby cried.

Meanwhile the other girls were having a great time. Gales of laughter pealed through the block. Anne Marie went outside to disperse the boys (brave girl), while I attempted to calm things down inside. The boys reluctantly wandered off into the darkness.

We insisted the girls went to bed and we put out the lights. Peace gradually fell, littered with the occasional giggle or sob.

What now? It was about 12.30 but Anne Marie and I weren't convinced the incident was over. We crouched down together just inside the doors to the block. Occasionally we heard someone whistling and calling to the girls. We'd jump up and tell them to go back to their tents. Then we'd crouch down again and wait for the next onslaught, ready to pop up at any moment. Fortunately the girls were all fast asleep, exhausted after their exciting evening.

And we were exhausted. We looked at each other and burst out laughing, hysterically, at the sheer madness of the situation. We couldn't laugh loudly for fear of waking the girls, so we just rolled around on the floor trying to stifle our giggles, which, of course, made the situation worse. You know what it's like when you try to stop laughing – a bit like corpsing on stage!

With tears running down our faces and with the realisation

that it was past two o'clock in the morning we decided to call it a night.

Four hours later, being woken by starving boys champing at the bit, we were *not* happy teachers. But you have to get on with it, I suppose. I couldn't have cared less whether Jonathon had dry toast or not!

The tents dried out and the girls moved back in. We mentioned the incident to the camp supervisor and thankfully we weren't bothered again.

Other memorable little snippets from that joyous week were the arrival of Mr Thomas with his newly-bought school cine camera and our free afternoon in Henley Town centre. The latter was highly amusing in retrospect. We took the children to Henley to buy some souvenirs. As all teachers know, the two things which create the most interest during any trips, day trips or lengthier ones, are eating and spending money. So we let them off the leash with instructions that they should meet us at a certain time in a set place.

Anne Marie and I took the opportunity to find a quaint little pub and had a delicious meal which we hadn't cooked on a camping stove. After the meal we walked along Henley High Street. Well turned-out ladies in twin sets and elegantly-attired gentlemen ambled from one delightful shop to another. Nannies pushed prams and chatted pleasantly with each other. It was a truly delightful scene - until we spotted Colin, one of our group. He was walking on all fours with a dog collar around his neck, which was attached to a lead held by Graham, another of our lads. Colin was barking at the ankles of the shoppers and occasionally whimpering when he was told off. He was having great fun. We looked at him, crossed the road and pretended he was nothing to do with us. Take a dog out of its kennel!

Tommy turned up on Thursday morning bright and breezy, camera in hand. It was pony-trekking day: a great photo opportunity. Always the technician, Tommy had it all in hand. He spent the morning filming us. Not surprisingly, the results were totally hopeless. Thirty seconds of unfocused footage and a great deal of blurred images. Obviously he later blamed the camera, not himself.

It had been a horrible experience for me. I realised that kids are absolutely fine during the school day, they were even all right if you had to be with them until six at clubs or competitions, but I knew after this experience that I desperately needed to go home every evening, to sleep in my own bed, to be in my own sanctuary. I managed to avoid all school journeys from that moment onwards.

Chapter 8

In my other life I had become a bit of a restless soul. During the summer holidays I had decided to have my long, Kate Bush-style curly hair cut. That had been a complete disaster. I cried when I left the hairdresser's and sobbed into my best friend, Linda's, chest. She suggested I went to see another friend of hers, who was a hairdresser. The only solution to such a bad haircut, she told me, was to cut it even shorter, which she did. This was a major life change! From cool rock chick to boringly ordinary chick took a lot of getting used to.

My third year of teaching began. On the first day, as luck would have it, I was on playground duty. I had the same class I had taught last year and so was regaled with hoots of laughter from the boys as I entered the playground because of my new 'look'. But it didn't take the class long to become familiar with the new me. After all, under the surface, I was still the same person.

Teaching was always interesting but it didn't always fulfil all my needs. Neither did my private life. I had met and had brief relationships with a few guys. Frank, whom I had known when living in Hammersmith years earlier, became a boyfriend for a while. He was a meteorologist with a First class Honours degree from U.C.L. We had a brief fling. He came round to my flat in Twickenham and all I can remember was that he wore a pair of shorts which allowed his tackle to hang free and in full view. My flat mate, Linda and I giggled so much about that.

He took me to a concert where The Who were due to play at a football ground in London. I wore a floor-length dress. The weather was foul. It rained almost constantly. I became completely fed up and wanted to go home long before The Who were due on stage, but escaping proved hazardous. As we attempted to make our way out, bottles and cans were aimed at us from all sides and the water seeped endlessly up my body.

At some point I went to his flat in Farnham. It was a fairly dull occasion. He left me for hours at a time, having been called away to work, and when he was there we entertained ourselves by throwing darts at a poster which showed different sexual positions. We tried two or three of them but it didn't do a lot for me. While Frank was out I got some paper and a pen and wrote several cryptic comments about the value of conversation and hid them all over the flat. He didn't find them while I was there, which is probably just as well, but I didn't see him again.

In the morning I had to drive from his place to school. My car wouldn't start! I was forced to wait over an hour for the AA to come and fix it. I rang school to explain, but I wasn't that bothered. In fact, it sort of rounded off a disastrous weekend.

I lived in Twickenham and would collect some of my colleagues on my way to school. Lindsay Maclean was my first pick up. Lindsay was interesting. She was 23, going on 50, and arrived at school at the start of my third year. She taught Design Technology and Cookery. She wore twin sets and fingerless gloves because her hands were always cold. She told me she had suffered continual sneezing bouts for two years whilst in her late teens. She didn't really drink, although I tried to change her ways by dragging her to the pub closest to school on Friday nights. I didn't succeed in getting her drunk, but I think she enjoyed the company while waiting for me as I was giving her a lift home.

It was indeed Lindsay who eventually succumbed to Bill's wiles. As time went by they began to form a relationship which must have satisfied both of their needs. Lindsay was very precise in everything she did. Everything had to be done 'just so' and you were in serious trouble if you didn't live up to her standards. She would make mincemeat out of the welfare staff who were there to support her. She would, perhaps unintentionally, humiliate children she didn't like and would occasionally make fun of their ethnic names. If she liked you, everything was fine but if she didn't... I understand that she went on to climb the teaching ladder and then became an independent consultant on certain areas of education. She had the drive I perhaps always lacked. But then I'd rather be me than her.

I picked Lindsay up on the way to school and continued to St Margaret's to pick up Diane, who didn't stay with us for long. One day, as I arrived at the meeting point for Diane, I turned off the engine to wait for her and when she arrived and I started the car nothing happened. Disaster! Here were three teachers with three classes to cover. What could we do?

We went back to Diane's, had several cups of coffee, waited for the AA man to arrive and eventually rolled up at school at about ten o'clock. The point here is that we were much more laid back. What else could we have done? We could have ordered a taxi which would have got us to school on time, but I don't think it occurred to any of us. This was an opportunity to chill out for a while. Even Lindsay didn't bat an eyelid. I became far more conscientious in later years.

My restlessness didn't go away. School was OK, it was fine, no problem, but it began to lack a challenge, whereas the world outside did. I wanted to travel, to experience something different. I was now in a fairly volatile relationship with a guy called John. When I mentioned to him that I wanted to leave teaching, he encouraged me and, at one time, I thought we'd go abroad together but it became apparent, as time went by, that this wasn't on the cards. When this realisation struck me I'd already handed in my notice and I was forced to make a decision about what I was going to do on my own.

I had friends who had gone to Israel and had worked on a kibbutz. This seemed like a good, safe option. I was going on my own and would have been stupid to hitch across Europe by myself, although I had done this many times with friends in the past. So the comparative security of a kibbutz was the best idea. I can't be philanthropic and say that I was going to Israel for any altruistic reason, as many young people, particularly Germans, did. It simply became a means to an end.

I asked Mr Thomas to write me a reference before I left. I was stunned by its brevity.

To whom it may concern
Miss E. M. D. Noakes

Miss Noakes was appointed to this school on 10th September 1974 from the list of First Appointments.

Miss Noakes satisfactorily completed her probationary year while teaching a 2nd year Mixed Middle School Class of children of 8-9 years of age.

Miss Noakes is a competent teacher now and has taught the 2nd and 3rd year age range successfully as a teacher of General Subjects.

Miss Noakes has a quiet but determined way with her pupils and has assisted with parent-teacher activities.

Miss Noakes is a very self-reliant person and has seldom need of help or assistance in any way, though she is always ready to listen to others.

Miss Noakes is most reliable in the performance of any administrative duties and we are sorry to lose her as a member of the staff. She has always been part of the team that has produced operatic and dramatic performances for parents.

Miss Noakes is well liked by her pupils, their parents and the staff. I can recommend her for the post for which she now applies.

If you do appoint Miss Noakes I am sure you will not be disappointed.

J W Thomas
Headmaster

My last year at school had gone well. I had great friends, enjoyed the bonhomie and I was relaxed and happy at school. Life was fine - except for a boy in my class called Jacob Sunderland. He had been difficult and disruptive and hadn't responded at all well to me. As a result I had seated him in a desk on his own at the front of the classroom. Today I would have placed him as far away from me as possible – you are far less able to notice or react to children who sit a long way away!

When his mum arrived for an open evening towards the end of the year she was extremely angry, claiming that her son had been ostracised from the rest of the class. She went to Tommy and said that she would have to do something about me. He apparently replied, 'Well, you'll have to find her first. She's going abroad!'

It was sad and not a little frightening to leave the school where I had been for the last three years. I'd made many friends and had great fun. On my leaving day I was given a £3 gift voucher from the staff! Even accounting for inflation I felt rather deflated. Apparently there had been no collection so I can only guess that this must have been how much Mr Thomas had valued me – no doubt he took it out of school petty cash. Kindly, my friends gave me individual gifts, which was lovely.

Chapter 9

At the beginning of September 1977, I found myself at Heathrow Airport, waiting for a flight to Tel Aviv. I was filled with apprehension. Why was I here? How had I got to this point? It had been a roller coaster. Somehow everything had been taken out of my hands. Having resigned, I had had to do something and I had to make some sort of decision. John had decided he didn't want to travel with me and I decided that Israel seemed the best option.

John came to see me off at the airport. I found it hard to say goodbye to him and to England. I went through the barrier and didn't look back. Israel was experiencing political difficulties in the 70s. I was given a body search (not unusual in those days) and my luggage was thoroughly checked. I had a suedette backgammon set which was taken away for scrutiny. It was given back to me an hour before flying. It appeared untouched, but I assume it had been scanned carefully for explosives or drugs.

Eventually we boarded the plane and I sat next to a girl who was due to meet a friend once we had arrived in Israel. She wasn't particularly friendly when I could have done with a friend. I felt very alone and not a little frightened. It was a

Boeing 747 jumbo and there were many Orthodox Hasidic Jews with ringlets and strangely fashioned black hats. I had never seen people like them before. Apparently there was a huge community in North London but not where I lived. As the pilot told us we were approaching Tel Aviv they all stood up and began to sing Hava Nagila.

The plane landed at such an unearthly hour of the morning that it was too early for the kibbutz office in Tel Aviv to be open, so I sat on my own on a chair in the airport waiting until the world woke up, wondering what on earth I was doing there. The airport was very quiet but gradually the sun came up and life began again.

I took a taxi into Tel Aviv and after many 'shaloms' managed to catch the correct bus to the kibbutz offices. Although only about nine o'clock, it was already hot. During the past two weeks the average temperature in Israel had been 37 degrees. I had a huge backpack and I'm not great in very hot weather.

I eventually left the kibbutz office with plans in place. I had been asked which kibbutz I wanted to go to. I could take my pick. A friend had given me the name of Hagoshrim, which he had been to, and since I didn't know anything about the others, I chose it. It was close to the border with Lebanon and the nearest town was Kiryat Shmona.

My plan was to head for the centre of Tel Aviv, where I would be able to catch a bus to the kibbutz. That's not quite how it turned out. As I plodded my way down the road in the heat, sinking under the weight of my rucksack, a middle-aged guy called out to me. He was really pleasant and we chatted to each other outside his flat. He asked me if I was thirsty, which I was, and he invited me in for a drink of water. It was good to meet a friendly soul. I was in no rush, so I accepted his invitation.

As it turned out he was a restaurant owner who lived in the flat during the week and returned to his wife and children at the weekend. He showed me a photo album of pictures of himself shaking hands with worldwide celebrities, including Harold Wilson. By this time he had found a few beers and we enjoyed them together.

By midday I was feeling slightly drunk, still very hot and quite tired. I hadn't slept much the night before. He kindly suggested that I could have a shower while he went into work for a couple of hours. He offered to take me to the bus station when I was ready. He showed me a single bed and said I could lie down for a while if I wanted to.

So he left and I took him up on his offer. When he returned I was asleep and it was late afternoon. He sat on the edge of the bed and woke me up. Then he kissed me, and then he did a great deal more. I recall crying and asking him to stop. I missed John, I was alone, and he was old and fat. It was horrible, but he didn't stop.

When it was over, he appeared completely normal. I hadn't screamed, I hadn't scratched or hit him. I was too numb to do anything. I kept thinking 'But he must be all right. I've seen the photographs.'

Very oddly, once it was over, he told me to get dressed and said that he would take me out for something to eat. And I went. Food didn't come from a posh restaurant. Instead he gave me a sight-seeing tour of Tel Aviv. We ate street food, which was tasty and very welcome.

It was now late. There was no chance of me travelling further. He took me back to the flat, where he now left me alone for the rest of the night. I can only think that he saw me as a willing participant in the sexual encounter we had had.

He returned the following morning and took me into the city. He even gave me a phone number. I never attempted to ring it, so I have no idea if it was false. I climbed onto the bus to Hagoshrim completely confused by the events that had taken place. There wasn't a lot I could do about it. He hadn't hurt me; in fact he'd been strangely kind and pleasant. I was even more confused than I had been when I left England, but I still had an adventure in front of me.

Following a fairly long journey I arrived at the kibbutz, where I was taken to meet Eliao, a lovely older gentleman who was in charge of the volunteer workforce. He introduced me to Pete, an English guy who had been on the kibbutz for six months and now had a certain status in that he was responsible for sorting out jobs for all the volunteers. Pete briefly showed me round the areas of the kibbutz where I was most likely to go. He was unattractive, tall and gangly, and he was neither friendly nor unfriendly.

The kibbutz was a rather pretty place. Lots of beautiful trees grew all over, providing a sweet scent. It had been founded in 1948, mostly by immigrants from Turkey. They had reclaimed the land and established a healthy, thriving community. The kibbutzniks lived in brick-built houses, while accommodation for the volunteers was rather more sparse – we had wooden huts all on one side of the kibbutz, hidden away from view. The kibbutz had a guesthouse where tourists stayed in comparative luxury and I think our accommodation was not part of a general tour of the site.

All food was provided free for us and we even received a token salary each week. Our clothes were washed for us once a week and we could buy cigarettes which were normally given to criminals in the prisons in Israel. They were very strong but very cheap! There was also a volunteers' 'pub' where we could buy cheap booze. The guesthouse prices were rather high!

I was shown to my 'hut'. Perfectly adequate accommodation; it had four beds and a toilet just outside. When I arrived two German girls occupied two of the beds and the other two were empty. It was the end of summer and the vast majority of the volunteers were students who had mostly travelled in pairs or in groups, so I was very much older and very much on my own. The volunteers were from many European countries including Holland, Sweden, Great Britain and a large group from Germany.

It took two weeks for letters to get home and equally two for replies to arrive, so it was a month before I had any contact with England.

My first letter to my mum said:

I am sharing a room with two German girls who aren't particularly friendly, or perhaps it's me. I start work tomorrow picking apples... I don't know how long I'll stay here at the moment. I feel like returning immediately.

I found it hard to make friends. I naturally gravitated towards the English-speaking volunteers but I think that as a single, older woman I was a bit of a threat. For many days I felt completely isolated and alone. I desperately needed some contact with home.

I hadn't even told my dad I was going to Israel. We had had a strained relationship for years. My parents divorced when I was 12 and, to begin with, I would travel from Northampton, where I lived with my mum and my brother, to London to see him about three times a year. He had always been a 'Victorian' father and I hate to think what would have happened if he had been around during my wild teenage years. He was a difficult man and I felt little affection for him. But such was my desperate need for someone to write to me that I decided to write and let him know what I was doing.

The reply I received contained the following:

Dear Eve,

It was certainly a surprise to learn that you are in Israel but if that is what you want to do so be it. You are certainly seeing a hard side of life and heavy by the sound of it to work hard as well, not that hard work did anyone any harm. It will all be a different way of life for you, how about the food is it tolerable? I do not like foreign food but there are many who do.

Love

Dad

He was right about the food. I was permanently ill, although not incapacitated. Since arrival at the kibbutz I had suffered stomach cramps and diarrhoea. This, I later acknowledged, was probably a symptom of stress. It usually happens whenever I am in an unfamiliar place or situation but this was the first time I had experienced it and I assumed I had some dreadful complaint. The spasms only happened straight after eating, so I virtually stopped eating altogether. It didn't happen after I'd had an alcoholic drink, so I consumed quite a lot.

The first letter I received from my mum was very different from Dad's. Amongst other things it said:

Dearest Eve,

I have been so worried because I had not heard from you, but today I received your letter which you wrote soon after getting to Israel. I don't know why it took so long… I hope by now things are better for you and that you have made some friends. I hope you are eating more as there won't be anything left of you… I do hope that there is no trouble with terrorists, it is rather frightening…

Lots of love

Mum XXXXXXXXXX

It was lovely to hear from her!

Chapter 10

My most regular job was apple-picking in the orchards. We had to get up at 4.15 in the morning (roused by Pete), because by midday it was too hot to work out in the sun. We all met in the communal canteen, where a quick breakfast was on offer, and then climbed into trucks which drove us out to the orchards. Once there, we were given large cloth-covered baskets which hung around our necks. The sun was beginning to rise and you could feel the heat in the air already. We were allocated rows and walked down each row collecting non-bruised apples from the floor. Once our baskets were full, we went to the end of the row, emptied them into a large container and continued. I suffered badly from the sun and the heat. The horse flies got to me and gave me huge bites, to which I reacted badly, but I carried on. There were a few times when Pete's call failed to rouse me and I slept in. No chance of being sacked here.

One of the most amazing and unfathomable sights I saw shortly after arriving was Brendan. As the name suggests he was Irish, red-haired and fair-skinned. The first time I met him a day after I arrived. He had been in Israel for two weeks. He was lying out in full sunlight with his shirt off. He had terrible blisters and sores all over his upper body, which were festering in the heat. This gave him no concern at all. I subtly suggested that maybe he needed medical attention, but he ignored my advice. A couple of days later he was forced to see a doctor and returned to Ireland very soon afterwards.

I also had a bad reaction to the sun for the first time. Previously, in England, I had simply turned a lovely shade of brown. In Israel all that happened was a terribly itchy rash over the areas I had exposed to the sun. While I watched from afar, many of the volunteers enjoyed the open air pool. I did take my towel down once and entered the pool tentatively. I felt very isolated and left quite quickly, possibly avoiding the ear infections from which many of the volunteers suffered.

I built up a bit of a relationship with Pete, who could see that I was flagging under the mid–morning sun. So my rota was changed. I now worked from about 4.30am until 8am in the orchard and was then taken back to the kibbutz. In the evening I worked at the guesthouse as a waitress, which was great and suited me much better. The kitchen was run by ladies from the local town of Kiryat Shmona. It was fascinating to see how they prepared the food in a kosher style. There were certain culinary rules, and since most of the tourists at that time were of Jewish origin, meals had to follow those rules. I had nothing to do with the preparation but simply delivered the food to the tables.

It was wonderful. The guests were very pleasant and kind and were also interested in me. They asked me questions about why I was in Israel. I didn't claim any noble reasons, but they didn't make any derogatory comments. It was lovely to be spoken to without the suspicion which I found from the other volunteers. I worked hard, I worked well and I enjoyed it immensely.

I was given tips, which was great, but these eventually became a bone of contention with the kitchen staff. They wanted me to share what I was given. I had little money and I began to hide my profits. Eventually, after about eight weeks, their annoyance at this led to me losing my job at the guesthouse, but I understood and simply relished the experience I had had there.

The kibbutz was very near the Golan Heights and there was sporadic bombing from the Lebanon. On one occasion while I was there three people were killed in Kiryat Shmona, only 3km away and, on another occasion, we were all rushed down the air raid shelter, where we had to wait more than three hours before we were allowed to leave. The shelter was horrendous. I didn't see any rats myself, but some volunteers claimed to have done so. There were beds with awfully dirty mattresses and the place smelt dreadfully musty. I don't think it had been used for some time and you could tell. However, we all made the most of it and the majority of us were excited rather than frightened.

The shelter proved useful on another occasion. After one evening shift in the Guest House I went to the bar and was having a beer with my English friend, Gerard, when John, an extremely tall (6ft 7ins) American guest whose table I had waited on earlier in the evening, arrived. He joined us and we began talking. I quickly developed a certain rapport with him. He was on his own at that time, whereas previously he had eaten with his wife and a group of friends. Gerard made his excuses and left. John's wife apparently had a migraine and I gathered their relationship was strained. We had a great time together and I offered to show him around the volunteers' area of the kibbutz, which, unsurprisingly, his group hadn't been shown on their official tour. It was a lovely evening, warm and fragrant, but as always I was aware of the constant prying eyes. There was nowhere to achieve any privacy - except the air raid shelter. Giggling madly, we went down there – it wasn't locked - and we continued to enjoy each other's company for quite some time. I did get several flea bites, but they were worth it!

John was leaving in the morning and I discreetly said goodbye to him. He sent me a letter from Tel Aviv which said:

> *Dear Eve,*
>
> *I wanted to write to you before we left Israel to tell you what a 'wild and wonderful' time I had with you. Air raid shelters are good for more than meets the eyes. The rates are reasonable and the service was elegant. Of all the places I've been in the last two weeks Hagoshrim will be most remembered... because of you.*
>
> *Love to you*
> *John.*

After the guesthouse, I was given a lot of other jobs. I picked quince, I worked sewing garments, I did whatever was required, but I missed my time serving meals at the guesthouse.

When October arrived many of the volunteers left, presumably to go back to universities. I was relieved and grateful, as it heralded a change. I'd been there for four weeks. During that time, for my sins, I hadn't behaved very well. Before I left England I had been told by Jimmy, a friend who had suggested I aim for Hagoshrim where he had spent some time, that a kibbutz was a bit like a knocking shop.

And so it proved to be. Being lonely and away from home, I took any opportunity to make friends. I was misguided and confused. I had several sexual experiences with guys from a range of countries, just to try to make myself feel worthwhile. It didn't work. I did like one particular guy, called Ingo, who was from Sweden. He reminded me of an old boyfriend, Tom, with whom I had had a three-year relationship at teachers' training college. Just like Tom, he was tall, with lots of fair hair, confident and funny.

Someone decided that the volunteers would put on a show for the kibbutzniks, and Ingo and I chose to enact a scene from *Joseph and his Technicolor Dreamcoat*. I was going to be Potipher's wife and Ingo was Joseph. We practised several times and went down a storm when we eventually performed to our public. We mimed the words to a record, which was good since I can't sing in tune, but we had choreographed the moves. I wore a very flimsy costume, which could have been why the crowd roared. With a feeling of euphoria, Ingo and I were feted by the audience, and when things died down we did the only thing a couple could do to celebrate their joint fame!

A trip had been arranged for the volunteers the next morning, and I wasn't entirely surprised to find that he had got up in time to join the party. I was too hung over and stayed in bed! We hardly spoke again and he reverted to the other friends he had made from his home country.

Gradually, as life and people in the kibbutz changed, I began to see the error of my ways – well for most of the time! I did have lapses.

Having boasted of my exploits to a close friend, Linda, I

received a letter from John, back in England, for whom I still had feelings. Unfortunately he had been with Linda when she had received a letter from me. She became increasingly embarrassed as she had to read it aloud to him. His reply said, amongst other things:

> *Dear Eve,*
>
> *I'm at Linda's house and have just read (twice) your most recent letter. I'm saddened. I really thought you'd use this almost ideal opportunity to put together all those good things that are you and just build up a little extra strength - the self-respect any of us need to hang on to what we believe. Self-respect is the basis of the strength needed to live life as we would wish to.*
>
> *Anyhow, I shouldn't preach. I don't think there's anything I could say that you don't know yourself.*
>
> *Do take care, please.*
>
> *Love and peace*
>
> *John XX*
>
> *PS Don't give Linda a hard time - it wasn't her fault I read the letter.*

It put me back on track. And then a really lovely guy called Gerard, who I've mentioned before, arrived at the kibbutz. I was in the volunteers' 'pub' reading *Zen and the Art of Motorcycle Maintenance*, which, at the time I thought held all the answers. He had left another kibbutz not far away, I never really found out why. But in a way he was my saviour and I was his. He had a horrible rash all over his face and I think was semi-literate. But I loved him entirely platonically, and as lost souls, we got on really well.

Instead of behaving badly, as I had done, Gerard became a soul buddy. We enjoyed each other's company and spent a lot of time together. There was absolutely no physical attraction on my side. He was just a nice, simple guy and I enjoyed being with him. Other volunteers often asked me if he was my boyfriend. I often did my own thing but he was always there when I needed him. When he left, before I did, I asked him to keep in touch, but he never did.

As time went by I began to resent the village community in which you couldn't do anything without everyone knowing, and I hadn't exactly been low profile.

I was very lucky in being offered a free tour of Israel by the kibbutz. This wasn't normally given to volunteers until they had been there for three months. I'd only been there for two. By this time two lovely Polish girls had moved into my hut. One of them had struck up a relationship with an Israeli guy called Izzy. It was very innocent and he was very sweet.

They all came on the trip. Once, when we were in Eilat, I foolishly asked an Arab on a camel for hashish. I could instantly see that I had said the wrong thing and I was saved when Izzy explained that I meant matches. Quick thinking and it was a close call!

At the same place I began to become bored with the company of my fellow volunteers so, as dusk approached, I decided to head off into the desert on my own. Crazy or what? It's not easy to walk through sand, but I plodded on and came across a group of European guys who had set up camp. They invited me to join them. They had some alcohol and we sat and talked for hours. Eventually I headed back to where we were camped, snuggled into my sleeping bag and went to sleep. I don't think anyone had missed me.

It was a fascinating journey. As I recall Jericho looked as if it hadn't changed since biblical days – people rode on donkeys through dirt streets and lived in inhospitable shacks. We were taken to the Dead Sea, where we were able to play in the salty waters without risk of drowning. We visited Masada, where we climbed up the mountain to see an amazing desert fortress overlooking the Dead Sea. It was a long, hard climb but well worth the experience once we reached the top. More poignant, was a visit to a Holocaust museum which was powerful in its recollections of the atrocities which the Jewish community had to endure during World War 2. It was spiritually stunning to see photographs of the torment which the Jewish people had to face and the humiliation before their deaths in the gas chambers.

I sent a letter home to my mum:

Jericho was a fascinating place - it reminded me a lot of Istanbul. It seemed as if the hand of progress had not touched it for 2000 years. Then we went down to the south of Israel - Nuweeba and Eilat. It was much hotter and we weren't far from the Sinai desert. The terrain remained the same for mile after mile. Very mountainous and barren. It gave you a strange feeling of space and freedom. There were beautiful white sands which stretched for mile upon mile, palm trees waving in the breeze, Arabs astride majestic camels and the clear blue sea lapping upon the beach. I loved the place and wished we could have stayed longer. We slept on the beach at night and I went wandering off on my own into the palms - Mmm!

As you may have gathered I hadn't really made many friends during my time in Israel, but there were two Scottish girls, Hazel and Marie, with whom I enjoyed spending time. They were also on the trip. On one day at about five in the afternoon Eliao called me over to him. He told me that there had been a fire at the kibbutz. The block of huts occupied by Hazel, Marie, Pete and another English volunteer, Steve, who hadn't been on the trip, had been virtually destroyed. Steve had raised the alarm but little of the building remained. He asked me how I thought the girls would take the news and whether I could tell them. They obviously only had left the things they had taken on the trip. I was slightly flattered that he had considered my opinion and help useful.

They took the news well and were given alternative accommodation when we returned to the kibbutz. The huts were certainly a terribly sad sight when we returned and looked at them. I think the implication was that with many of the volunteers away, some young Israelis had deliberately set fire to them. Everyone was very philosophical about it. There was no insurance and no one was recompensed.

Chapter 11

And so we returned to Hagoshrim. Another very sad event had happened during the few days we had been away. A gorgeous dog, which we named Scruffy, because he was, had become a companion to many of the volunteers. He was playful and very affectionate and would often be found lying on the grass outside my hut surrounded by groups of volunteers. Everyone loved him. Apparently Scruffy had turned up one day behaving very aggressively, slavering at the mouth and running round in circles. The remaining volunteers had tried to help but were told to stay in their huts. Someone arrived and shot Scruffy. We were told that he had probably been bitten by a wild animal which had rabies. Poor Scruffy.

It was now mid-November and life continued in much the same vein. Gerard continued to be a great friend, but decided to go home before the end of the month. He wanted to be a landscape gardener. I don't know if he ever fulfilled his ambition. He gave me his address and I did write to him but, as I said, never received a reply. I'm not sure he could write!

So, more or less alone again, although generally happy, I decided I should visit Jerusalem. After all you can't be in Israel without visiting, arguably, its most historic place. I caught a bus from Kiryat Shmona and arrived in Jerusalem in the late afternoon. I found a hostel close to the Damascus Gate and settled myself into an adequate room which was already occupied by three other travellers.

Once settled, I took myself off for a walk around the old city. I loved it. It was a mixture of Arabs and Israelis and, of course tourists. I visited the Wailing Wall and was fascinated by the sheer history of it all.

When I returned to the hostel, my room-mates told me they were going to a disco and asked if I'd like to come. It seemed a little incongruous going from a place steeped in history to a modern disco, but I went. It was fun, with flashing lights, loud music and lots of dancing.

A new day dawned and I thought a bit of window-shopping was a good idea. I didn't have any money to spend, but I could at least look. As the custom remains in many foreign places today, if you were obviously a tourist you were targeted and hassled. I found it quite fun, the bartering and the banter. I was looking in one particular shop which sold jewellery when an extremely tall and handsome young Arab began the usual conversation. He took me into the shop, sat me down, offered me tea and began to show me a range of necklaces, bracelets and earrings. I told him I couldn't afford anything, but he was good eye candy and I fancied him. I sat down in a very comfortable seat while he went about his job. He wasn't the owner of the shop. He and another guy handled the selling while the boss man dealt with the money side.

Eventually I think the boss got tired of my presence and told

Jack (presumably an Anglicised name) to get rid of me. Jack suggested going to a bar for a drink and I couldn't have been happier, although I don't think the attraction at that time was mutual. I obviously paid for the drinks and Jack clearly had a lot of friends of all nationalities. He was able to converse in a range of languages. There was a pretty girl from Sweden who was obviously very keen but I stuck it out and amused him with silly mind puzzles that I knew. The Swedish girl left.

Jack suggested going to a friend's house somewhere in Jerusalem. When we arrived there was copious alcohol and Jack drank more and more. We ended up having sex. In no way could it be described as making love. It was mechanical, aggressive and without feeling.

When we woke the following morning Jack took me back to the hostel and invited me to meet him again that evening. From such an inauspicious start we began to build a relationship. I liked him and he grew to like me. He told me of his family, with whom he didn't have a great relationship, and the hopelessness of his life as an Arab in Jerusalem. He had spent some time in Switzerland but had been deported. He was a 'bad lad' and had been in trouble with the police, but I became very fond of him. There was a deep sexual attraction and when we could afford it, we stayed in cheap hotels for the night. I received some very strange looks from hotel staff (a European girl with an Arab) but I didn't care.

I was in Jerusalem for a week and we spent most of the time together. Apart from his job in the shop, he had a little workshop of his own where he made jewellery. I would sit there watching him and talking about my life in England.

At the end of the week I returned to Hagoshrim possibly more despondent than ever. That was when I made the decision to return to England. Israel had been an interesting experience, but the kibbutz life, I was absolutely sure, wasn't for me. I needed freedom, I needed my friends, and I missed my life in England. I made plans for my return.

But before that happened I wanted to go back to Jerusalem to see Jack again. I booked my return ticket to England and at the same time booked a ticket back to Jerusalem, leaving me five days to be with Jack. Hazel decided that she was also ready to go home, so we travelled back to Jerusalem together.

I can't honestly say that I had any regrets in leaving the kibbutz. Maybe the only thing it had taught me about myself was that I hated the closeness of such a small community. No, that's not entirely true. I discovered how difficult it was for me to make friends and the lengths to which I would go to change this. I had been reckless and not a little bit desperate at times, but I had come through on my own and had survived with my sanity and my life intact.

Hazel and I booked into the hostel but in fact I saw little of her. I spent the time with Jack. My belongings, on one occasion without my permission, had been moved from one four-bedded room in the hostel to another in which about eight guests slept on the floor. I wasn't there that much, so I didn't care. When Jack wasn't around during the day I went to view the sights. The Marc Chagall stained glass windows at the Jerusalem hospital were stunning as the light fell on them. I never made a trip to Bethlehem but was told that it was rather a letdown in any case.

Jack and I continued to relate to each other very well. He

came up with the idea that he would make lots of jewellery which I could take back to England and sell, then send the money back to him so that he could come and join me in England. It seemed like a good plan to me and here in a foreign land anything seemed possible!

So I sat for hours and watched as he made his jewellery. An old guy came up to me one day when Jack was working at the shop and I was waiting in his workshop for him. He offered me some tea, which I accepted. That evening Jack told me that the old man was most upset because I hadn't paid him. It hadn't occurred to me. I thought he was just being friendly. A different world!

Jack explained how to get the jewellery through customs legally and I gave him promises that I would do my best to sell it all, which I sort of did.

My flight home was timed for 11am. I didn't ring to check until the morning of departure, when I discovered that the flight time had been changed and I had missed it. I had been with Jack the night before. My bag was packed with his jewellery and he had seen me off in a taxi to the airport, with promises of what life might hold in the future.

But the plane had gone and the airport was deserted. The authorities arranged for me catch a flight to Amsterdam where I would have to transfer onto a flight to Heathrow. What a to-do.

I received a letter from Hazel when I was back in England in which she wrote:

On Sunday I phoned the airport and they informed me of the cancellation of the 11 o'clock flight and put us both down for the 9 o'clock. We found the number of the youth hostel to try and tell you about the change, but we couldn't get through and I thought you would phone anyway.

If only I had. No mobile phones in those days!

I also received a letter from Jack – actually several over the next six months. We had been somewhat carried away with our relationship and Jack was very keen to come to live with me in England, hoping the earrings would be a way in which he could earn some money. When reality hit, along with the cold light of day, I realised that this was extremely unlikely to happen.

His first letter was sweet:

Eve

Hello. I hope you are doing fine.

Right after you left Israel in four days I started waiting for the post every day. Soon I received your letter and I was glad to hear from you.

I was always doing nothing here not even working because I always waited for your letter. I'm waiting for a letter to tell me what to do, so tell me how the earring business is going on with you and tell me if I have to send more of them so I can do it.

Eve, it is Jack who is writing you, be sure that Jack now is a different person do you believe that I did not drink since six days, I don't even stay out late at night, even on Christmas evening. I didn't even go to Bethlehem for the first time I spend my

Christmas time with my family at home and for the first time after six or seven days I drank two glasses of wine with my father and believe me that's all. You cannot imagine how much happy my mother feels because I go home early.

I hope that you were here on Christmas, so we would have had really nice time together, but you remember when I promise you not to go out with any girl, I still keep my promise and I controlled myself even on Christmas eve. my friends invited me to go out with them, but I said no and I stayed at home as I told you.

Tell me, do you often think of me as I do? You cannot imagine how serious I'm getting from day to day. I get more and more serious of what I always told you I want to do with you, I always waited your letter. Please try to write often and tell me what is going on with you so I can send some more stuff because I am in a hurry I want to come as soon as possible. I stop now but I'll be writing more. I miss you; A big hug to you. Write soon. I'll see you soon

With love

Jack XXXX

I honestly did make an effort to sell the earrings. I trundled them around shops and markets in West London, but I wasn't very good at it and sold very few. Over time he became increasingly worried about my lack of success and increasingly frantic. I had to let him down slowly and eventually his letters stopped.

Chapter 12

———✄———

Settling back to life in England wasn't easy. I stayed with friends and tried to steer clear of falling back into teaching, but what else could I do? It seemed very little, and certainly nothing that would give me anything close to the salary I had been receiving. I tried my hand at selling insurance and savings plans exclusively for women – WISP. I had a week's training up in London and the first task was to deliver 1000 fliers, trudging the streets and climbing up huge high-rise blocks of flats. Well, that was enough to make me think again and I gave up before I had even begun.

What to do now? I had been back in England for about four months. I had really outstayed my welcome with friends and I knew this couldn't go on. So I did what most people do, I went home to Mummy.

Mum lived with my stepfather, Jack, in Northampton. I'd been claiming the dole since I'd returned from Israel. When I reached Northampton I went for an interview at the job centre and the only job they could offer me was as a prison officer. Scary and no, thank you. By this point I was realising that I would probably have to go back to teaching, but ironically I couldn't get a teaching job in Northampton unless I was already working for the borough. How strange was that? Catch 22.

I decided I had to do something. I saw an advert in the local paper inviting people to audition for the open air production of Othello in Abington Park. I went along to the audition and, as an outsider, I think I quite surprised the casting team. There aren't many female parts in Othello, but I was offered the role of Bianca. Rehearsals started and I enjoyed them. The play was set to be performed for five nights in the Open Air theatre in Abington Park during July.

As it happened the weather was dreadful all week. We only completed one entire performance, with all the others being cancelled at some stage during the performances. I had met a schoolboy called Andrew who had a small part in the play, and we had a little non-sexual liaison. I recall that I went round to his house one day after rehearsals and we were chatting in his room when his mum came in. I think she was horrified that I was clearly much older than him - she was certainly very frosty. I picked him up one day from school. That must have made waves amongst his school mates!

On the last day of the performance there was a party. Some of us ended up staying the night at the house of Gary, who played Iago. When I got back to Mum and Jack's house in the morning, they had contacted the police to say that I was missing. I was furious. I didn't even consider that I should have phoned them. I was used to doing my own thing in London and having no one to answer to. Obviously, with hindsight, I behaved badly. I should have let them know, but this incident illustrated the fact that I couldn't live at home any more.

During the rehearsals I was offered a job at Daventry Teachers' Centre, where I was to be in charge of a team of six people making resources for health education. They were a lovely group of girls and I did begin to build up a relationship with them. Ironically, because I was now employed by Northampton, I began to be offered supply teaching jobs which were far more lucrative than the job at the teachers' centre.

It was May and I enjoyed teaching in a range of schools, both in the centre of Northampton and out in the countryside. At one middle school I was amazed to find the teacher who had taught me Biology at High School. In another rural school it was great to take my class to see sheep-shearing but I longed to be back in London. I had always said that the best place in Northampton was the railway station, because it meant you were getting out of there.

During June I applied to be a supply teacher back in Hounslow and was offered work. My brother Ken let me stay with him and his family. I taught in a school in Chiswick which had many children whose parents were working for foreign embassies. I taught in schools in Feltham where the kids loved their teacher but hated me. I taught middle-class children and working-class children. But I never really enjoyed supply teaching, because there was never any time to build a relationship with the class. I am aware that many teachers love supply teaching. No planning, no staff meeting, no ties. It wasn't for me.

I was still in touch with the teachers at my previous school who had remained when I left and I was told that a part-time special needs teacher was needed from September 1978. They were termed remedial teachers then. I had no experience whatsoever of teaching children who required help with English other than those who had been members of my own classes. I applied for the job and was invited to an interview with Mr Thomas and a representative from Ealing council. She asked me what experience I could bring to the job and a pause followed. Mr Thomas, God bless him, said 'I'm sure Miss Noakes would be only too happy to attend the necessary courses,' and, of course, I concurred. I was given the post.

I taught small groups throughout the middle school and used whatever resources were available in school to teach them. I enjoyed being back in the same school and I loved the work. There is a different relationship when you are only teaching small groups. The children were more relaxed and, at that time, were grateful for any help they could receive. I would take groups for half an hour and then return them to their classrooms before collecting the next group.

At least that was the idea. One day I took a group at 9.00 while the rest of the school had assembly. I could see their classroom from where I was teaching, so I waited until I saw the rest of the children coming back from assembly. On this particular day there were no children returning by 9.45, 10.00, 1015… eventually I saw the class at 10.30. Mr Thomas had done another of his epics. The poor children had been sitting on a hard floor in the hall for 90 minutes! I was told later that Mr Thomas was explaining to the children, amongst other things, 'Fish do not have fingers and cod do not have balls'. Apparently there was a lot of restrained sniggering amongst Year 7.

Since this was only a part-time job, I had to continue supply teaching. I had no problem finding daily work and the best part was being able to decide, on occasions, that I didn't want to work on a particular day. The pay, pro rata, was very good. You didn't have to pay agency fees then. Gary Bates, a head teacher and friend of my brother, rang me one evening to ask if I would come and do some supply teaching at his school the following day. I knew of the reputation of the school. It was in a rough area of Hounslow and the kids were known to be difficult. I remember saying 'Oh no Gary, I can't do that. I'll be eaten alive'. He reassured me and, with huge apprehension, I drove to the school the following day. I knew Gary well socially and didn't want to fail in his eyes. He was very supportive. I had a second-year class who were lovely and a fourth-year class who were under threat of death from Gary if they put a foot wrong. It was a good experience and went really well.

Early in the spring term, Penny announced that she was to be married to an Irish guy whom she had met at a mutual friend's wedding in Dublin. We were all delighted. She was a lovely, innocent girl who didn't have a bad word to say about anyone; a great innovative teacher who was liked by all. Unfortunately, not long after the announcement of her engagement, she discovered that he was not the man she thought him to be. He was already engaged to another woman! Such was her embarrassment that she decided to resign, unable to cope with the situation she found herself in.

I was offered the opportunity to take over her job as a full-time teacher of a first year class – in those days 7-8 year olds. I went into her classroom to meet the children. Quietly she pointed out a particular little boy of West Indian origin and said, 'He's a cute one.' I knew that she meant he was a little pest. He overheard and when I took over the class he would delight in saying, 'I'm the cute one.' Anything but! We were all sad to see Penny leave, although many of the staff never discovered the real reason for her departure.

There had been many changes since I began at school. Gill Last, a young and very enthusiastic teacher, had arrived. She later became one of my best friends. Tess Morgan was new to our school, although she had taught before in High Schools. Tess became my soul buddy until her untimely death in 2009.

Sylvia Flint and Gill King, who had both begun teaching a year before I arrived, were still there. They both had a very imperious attitude over the younger staff and tended to intimidate them. To us they presented a united front although they were, in fact, very different people. Sylvia was married to Andy and as far as I could see they led a very safe, somewhat boring, lifestyle. Sylvia used to knit in the staff room. Gill, on the other hand, as I discovered later, was a much more interesting character. Married to Kelvin, a solicitor, she led a wild lifestyle, clubbing and partying with a wide range of straight and gay friends.

Hilda Duveen had been at the school when I had arrived. She was a lovely, intelligent, eminently sensible lady in her fifties. She was married to a gentleman called Vin. His real name was Adolf but being Jewish and living through the Second World War in Holland, he had understandably changed his name. Vin would never talk about the war and I suspected that he must have endured some terrible times and experiences.

I was the only one of the probationers who had begun teaching in 1974 who was still there. Two Kathys had arrived. One was Kath Barrett, who had decided to become a teacher after starting a family. She must have been in her early thirties. She was a feisty character, very strong-willed and great fun. Kath, being older, would often stand her ground when challenged by Tommy and as a consequence he was a little more wary of reprimanding her. She would not be afraid of standing up to him and we admired that.

The other, Kathy Kickham, was young and joined us from college. I have to admit that she drove me insane at times. She would come into my classroom on several occasions, look at the wall displays and hey presto, the same displays would suddenly appear on her classroom walls. Kathy stayed with us for a few years and when I last heard of her, she had become an advisory teacher in another area of England. Let's hope I helped her on her way.

Chapter 13

— ✕ —

That spring term proved to be an interesting one, historically, in Southall. I had moved into an unfurnished flat above a butcher's shop in the older part of Southall, a 20-minute walk from school but thankfully outside the immediate catchment area. Southall was fascinating. Although I'd taught there for some time I now had the opportunity to experience the true life of the town. Essentially Southall was split into two main areas, the old part centred on King Street and the newer part which surrounded the Uxbridge Road.

I loved walking around watching the ladies shopping in their saris, the smell of a wealth of spices issuing from the restaurants and cafés. Shops sold colourful material at ridiculously cheap prices, endless gold jewellery and pots and pans I'd never seen the like of. Southall was a truly mixed community. With its close proximity to Heathrow airport, it had become the new home to a wide range of ethnic groups. There was a large West Indian community, Asian Sikh and Hindu communities, Ugandan Asians thrown out by Idi Amin and much later Southall became home to Somali immigrants and Eastern European economic migrants.

We taught racial tolerance actively at school and expected the children to respect each other's religious and cultural beliefs. The 'Christian' assembly had to change and Mr Thomas slowly altered the focus for these. Classes would take assemblies, opening up the opportunities for the children to learn from and about each other.

However, increasingly, there was animosity in many parts of England fired by the words of the MP Enoch Powell, who ignited prejudice and intolerance. In his 'Rivers of Blood' speech in 1968 he had said, 'In this country in fifteen or twenty years' time the black man will have the whip hand over the white man' and there were many racists who believed him.

Things came to a head in Southall on April 23rd (St George's Day), 1979. A meeting of National Front members was to take place at Southall Town Hall attended by a small number of agitators intent on inciting racial hatred. These were not residents of Southall but had been deliberately brought to the area to cause trouble.

The police were out in force, as it was clear the situation was volatile. They had cordoned off the area leading to the Town Hall to block anti-racism demonstrators from attempting to disrupt the meeting. Hundreds of demonstrators of many nationalities living in Southall stormed the police barricades, and, in the confrontation that followed (which was extremely violent) a 33-year-old teacher called Blair Peach was brutally killed by the police.

The following day, of course, the older children were buzzing with the news and with accounts of what had happened to older siblings and members of their families who had witnessed or been involved in the events of the previous evening. We tried to calm them down but allowed them to talk quietly to us if they needed to. I think the children knew that we, as teachers, had always shown understanding and respect for their cultures and, although we were all white and of British origin, we had no tolerance or sympathy for the pro-racist beliefs of the National Front.

In its way that terrible night united us as a school, and indeed our country, in the belief that racism would not be tolerated.

There were other later riots in Southall in the 1980s. I had met Robert, who was later to become my husband. He lived in Brixton. Ironically one day the butcher whose shop I lived above told me that there was likely to be trouble that evening in Southall and suggested I stay somewhere else that evening. I rang Robert and caught the tube over to Brixton, only to be met by rows of riot police there too. Out of the frying pan into the fire!

And so I settled back into life at G.T. I can't say that I had laid my demons to rest, had gone forth, explored and was now happy to settle down. I still kept in touch with John Hamilton, who was now in Australia, and we sent letters back and forth planning for me to emigrate under John's sponsorship. I contacted the Australian embassy, but when we discovered he would have to marry me within three months of my arrival, and we both realised we were drifting apart, our letters became less frequent and eventually petered out.

At the end of the summer term, as usual, the classes for the following academic year were arranged. I was to teach the 8-9-year-old classes alongside Gill Last. We arranged to meet towards the end of the summer holidays to plan for the autumn term. When we met I asked Gill how her holidays had been, and was devastated when she told me her father had died suddenly. He had driven home, turned off the car's engine and suffered a heart attack before getting out of the car. Gill was incredibly close to both her mum and her dad and this had obviously come as a complete shock. He was only in his late 50s. I'd met him once or twice when he had picked Gill up from school and he seemed such a lovely man.

Gill and I worked brilliantly together. We had a great rapport and a very similar method of teaching. The children in our classes, which were next door to each other, would easily intermingle for different lessons and Gill and I would often be found in each other's classrooms. Such was our relationship with each other that the children didn't seem to mind who was teaching them. We sent silly messages with the children. One day I sent a million-pound cheque to Gill. The kids were astounded and fascinated and loved it, guessing what Gill could spend the money on - a set of lessons in itself!

I had a little girl called Rashmi in my class. She spent most of the day crawling underneath the desks. She shouldn't have been in mainstream school, had no individual support, and I just coped with her as best I could. She wasn't aggressive or disruptive; we just got used to her. By the end of the year she had moved to a special school. Today she would have remained in mainstream with 1:1 support.

Gill joined me in running the extra-curricular gymnastics club which I had previously run with Anne Marie. We loved seeing how quickly the children, both boys and girls, progressed.

Gill was brilliant at teaching them to vault well over the box. Handsprings, headsprings, straddles, long arm over swings: we had great success. I found it quite frightening as we pulled the springboard further and further away from the box in order to produce fantastically well-performed vaults. I was always inclined to be too close, to protect the children, while Gill had more faith, justifiably, in their ability. We would both choreograph their floor sequences, linking six moves together which flowed dynamically. We became quite obsessed for a number of years and were immensely proud when we won the all-Ealing gymnastic competition. Unlike many other schools we didn't have many children who went to gym clubs and most learnt their talents directly from us.

One Sunday we attended a course at a local High School, along with many other teachers, to gain a BAGA (British Amateur Gymnastics Association) coaching award. We were shown how to teach some quite complex moves and then we were all taken into a room to sit a written exam. We were actively encouraged to help each other with the answers while the examiners left the room. I can't imagine that anyone failed unless they were hearing–impaired, as we all loudly discussed the answers. The strangest test I'd ever sat.

The P.E. courses run by Ealing were easily the best and most useful in terms of demonstrating how to teach the many diverse areas of the P.E. curriculum. They were nearly always run by Jim Hall, who was an inspiration. Full of energy and enthusiasm, he taught us how to motivate and encourage the children to enjoy a wide range of physical activities. He would come into school and teach classes, amazing the children by walking on his hands.

While doing this once at our school, all his money fell out of his pockets. I had never seen the children move so quickly to pick it up. I'm sure he got almost all of it back.

Gill and I, as I have said, worked well together. We would take great pride in producing beautiful art displays in the hall and corridors, double-mounted and colour-matched. We had the time – no planning to do and very few meetings to attend.

At Christmas we were asked to create Santa's grotto in the science room which was only used for science lessons - Bunsen burners, test tubes - very high school! The cupboard in the science room contained ghoulish bottles of preserved parts of creatures. Anyway, prior to the evening's Christmas event we gathered together a range of materials for the job. I don't know how, but neither of us had our classes and we were able to get on with the job. We hung netting across the ceiling and attached it delicately to pivotal points. On to the netting we pinned twinkling stars and used lametta and cotton wool to create a wintry effect. It was all progressing very well until suddenly Mr Thomas and Lindsay turned up. She wanted to have a choir rehearsal in the Science room, which meant that everything would have to be dismantled. I couldn't believe it. But she was Tommy's golden girl and what Lindsay wanted, Lindsay got.

'Right,' I said with venom in my voice, 'OK, no problem,' and I began, in fury, to pull all our hard work to pieces. The look of fear on Tommy's face was the only saving grace and I swear that from that day onward I went up enormously in his estimation. Once her half-hour rehearsal was finished we put it all back again.

At the end of that year Jeff Trott escaped Mr Thomas' rigidity.

He had consistently tried to stand up to Tommy but had consistently failed. He took a sideways move, returning as deputy head to the school he had previously left to join us. I think it was just a relief to get out.

Dave Price was to replace him. I recall meeting Dave in July at the local watering-hole after school. After congratulating him I advised him that to make a success of his job, he would be best never to cross Tommy, never to support us and never to suggest changes to Tommy's way of doing things which were entrenched in the 1960s. As it happened he didn't need my advice.

Chapter 14

During the summer holiday, despite the fact that I was now 28, I went on holiday with Mum and Jack to Malta. Just shows how desperate I was. It was a pleasant but somewhat boring holiday for the most part. Always conscious of safety, I hid my passport under the mattress of my bed in the apartment where we stayed. We enjoyed some sightseeing and some days on the beach. Malta had a lot of beach boys who were essentially there to rip off the tourists. When we were having a pre-dinner drink, Francis began talking to us. He wasn't as young as most of them and he was quite sweet.

Francis and I struck up a friendship and I spent quite a bit of time with him, which was preferable to spending time with the oldies. He took me to a race track where, for fun, lads brought their souped-up cars and raced each other at breakneck speed up and down the track; a bit like in the film 'Grease'. We stood and watched. We didn't take part, I'm pleased to say. It was quite exhilarating.

When it was time to go home, Francis offered to drive me to the airport for our departure flight and I arranged to meet Mum and Jack there - which was fine, except that I left my passport under the mattress! I didn't realise until we had arrived at the airport, and there was no time to go back for it. Actually I would have been quite happy to stay a while longer in Malta. However, the authorities were very understanding and I was allowed to travel home without a passport – I wasn't that relieved. I said goodbye to Francis and, of course, said I'd go back, which I never did.

Francis wrote several letters to me. The first said, and this is exactly as it was written:

My Dear EVE

Well I told you that I would write and I hope you will write Back, when you lefat me I wase started to cry cause I was lucky to meet you. I hope you well sand me A photo of you love,

EVE is that true you are coming on October. Do you really think you will be coming over to Malta. I hope you or coming back to me.

Please Please write back

And soon

I will think of you until we meet again so we have to finish the Bacardi

See you love

I hope you lock this writing

See YOU XXXXXX

My Dear

This is true

I never stoll botels from a bar never have I hope you belevme cous as I told to you for you to be happe ok.

He also sent me a poem, which wasn't bad considering his grasp of English wasn't that great.

On the flight home I sat apart from Mum and Jack and was amazed when the air steward brought me a bottle of champagne – a large bottle! 'This is especially for you,' he told me. Well I knew it wasn't from Francis. He would never have been able to afford it. As the flight continued I could tell that the cabin crew were talking in hushed voices about me. The steward, who was very handsome, passed by me and I grabbed his attention.

'This wasn't meant for me, was it?' I said.

He smiled and replied, 'Um, no. It was a mistake but don't worry. Just enjoy it!'

Which I did! I also enjoyed standing chatting to him and the other cabin crew and even put up with chronic earache, due to cabin pressure, without batting an eyelid. I gave him my address and he did write to me. I met him when he had a stop-over in London. It was a complete disaster, as we had absolutely nothing in common, and I never saw him again.

All too soon the autumn term began. I was in the classroom closest to Mr Thomas' room and the Middle School offices and staffroom. I liked this because I could see everything that was going on. I've always been nosey.

Dave Price had joined us now as deputy head and we had two other male teachers, Mike Barnard and Richard Franklin.

Mike was a fascinating character. He was in his late 30s, wore a black cape, a trilby and played the saxophone with a band in the evenings and at weekends. He was a loose cannon. He smoked cigarettes in his classroom during the breaks and at lunchtimes. His philosophy was 'Do as I say, not as I do.' At the end of the year he wrote on a child's report, 'He has the co-ordination of a drunken camel.' Needless to say it didn't go home in that form.

Richard was young, thin and handsome. He was a great guy and an amazing shot. He used to flick chalk across the classroom to hit a child who was talking or not paying attention. His aim was legendary. I had a bit of a crush on Richard. I think all the young female staff did. Socially he kept himself to himself. He would occasionally come for a swift half, but not often. He stunned all of us when, after he had been at school for about three years and we were having an end-of-term staff lunch, he nipped off-site and returned with his partner and his little baby son. None of us had any idea. I would love to have seen our faces.

Dave began to settle in to his new post. A quietly-spoken Welshman, he began to find his feet. Very soon after he started, in October, I noticed some strange activity around Tommy's room. Janet, the secretary, went in and out of his room. Dave appeared and Tommy's door was firmly closed, which was odd because it wasn't his usual nap time. Then I saw the paramedics and it was at this point that I realised something was really amiss. I closed the classroom door to stop the little beady eyes, which missed nothing.

It transpired that Tommy had suffered a serious stroke. His wife arrived and he was taken to hospital. Word soon spread amongst the staff and we were all in shock. I cannot imagine how Dave felt. Here he was, an inexperienced deputy head a month into his new job, having to hold the reins, albeit temporarily.

It became clear that Tommy would not be returning to us soon. Ealing Education Department realised that Dave was not experienced enough to take over as acting head and so Claire Campbell arrived. I used to refer to her as 'Jolly Hockey Sticks'. She was one of those heads who go where they are most needed when they are needed. She was in her fifties, wore tweed and flat shoes. I didn't like her much. She was very masculine and very matter of fact, determined to get her own way.

In retrospect she was probably exactly what the school needed although it didn't feel like that at the time. Miss Campbell was, I think, horrified by what she found at our school when she arrived and set about changing things. As a staff we had bumbled away, mostly left to our own devices, and had previously not had to account for what we were doing in our classrooms just as long as we didn't use too many resources. Miss Campbell had different ideas.

I have to admit that the textbooks in the school were nearly all 20 or 30 years old and most were falling to pieces. She threw them away and ordered new ones. She was constantly checking in classrooms to see what was going on. You could hear her stomping down the corridor. I wasn't part of the management team of the school, so I don't really know the full impact or influence of what she did in her brief time at the school. She wasn't approachable but just seemed to bark her commands at us. However, she supported and encouraged Dave enormously and no doubt he learnt a great deal more from her with regard to good practice than he would ever have learned from Tommy.

Mr Thomas did return to school in June of the following year, but it was clear to all of us that he could not continue in his role of Head Teacher. In assemblies he found it hard to climb the steps on to the stage. His speech was still slurred and he was clearly unable to carry out the various roles of a head teacher.

The powers that be decided that the job should be advertised. I have no idea how this was handled. I do know that Dave continued to visit Mr Thomas and his wife regularly for a considerable time until Mr Thomas' death some years later.

A short list was drawn up and Dave was on it. And, to his amazement, just a year after he had secured the deputy headship, he was offered the job! Speaking to him later, in fact at my retirement, he said that it had been a huge shock and in no way had he been ready for such responsibility. It didn't seem that way to us. We liked Dave and he never showed us that he was unable to cope with the job. He was a quiet, self-contained man who rarely showed his true feelings to the staff of his school. He was always supported by Chris, his wife, who was also a teacher and I think a soulmate who he could talk to and gain confidence from.

Chapter 15

Obviously with Dave's appointment as head teacher, a vacancy existed for a new deputy head. John Maxwell arrived with a flourish. John had trained initially as an architect and then retrained as a teacher. He had been teaching in a middle-class school in a fairly privileged part of Ealing where his willingness to involve himself fully in the life of the school, especially in terms of extra-curricular activities, had been noticed by the borough. John had been actively encouraged to apply for deputy headships, although he was quite happy to stay where he was.

John was in his late twenties. He lived with his mother and brother in Harrow. He was a Catholic, although this in no way affected his teaching except that he had a very established moral code. He had a lively social life which revolved around a theatre group, of which he was a very active member. John was also a musician, although he claimed he couldn't really read music very well. However, he kept us entertained for many, many years writing plays which he produced and directed for the children, who performed to a very high standard. He would instinctively recognise and nurture talent in children who perhaps were unable to succeed in other areas of school life.

John was allocated a very lively class of 11 and 12-year-olds. John and Dave complemented each other perfectly. John was the showman, with hundreds of fabulous ideas to use with the children. He was very much involved directly with the children, always suggesting ways in which to make their experiences at our school happy and unforgettable. Dave worked diligently behind the scenes ensuring the plethora of management tasks were tackled effectively.

John would be the 'front man' and Dave would be brought in on more serious occasions if the children needed to be admonished by their head teacher. Dave dealt with the parents and was greatly admired by them once he had established himself. He had a real talent when mentoring both the children and their parents during private interviews, and would do all he could to improve the quality of their lives.

They were a team and John would always defer to Dave when it was necessary. There was great respect from both sides.

John brought many new things with him: 'Fun Morning', the staff panto, sports days, inter-house quizzes and much more. He invigorated all of us - staff and children alike.

We were still a Middle School and within his class John had two lads, Graham Stacey and Joel Denton, younger brother of my sometime nemesis Johnny. They were lovely boys who had a very healthy sporting rivalry. Joel was quite self-contained: Graham was very different. At eleven his voice had already broken, and he possessed a well-tuned muscular physique in advance of his years. I taught him gymnastics after school. He showed great talent. I recall on one occasion when we were practising vaults for a performance that he hit the springboard awkwardly and hurt his foot. He made no fuss and carried on training. However, it transpired that he had broken a toe! His mum took him to hospital, but he still turned up that evening to support the other children although, of course, he couldn't perform himself.

Graham would often turn up at my classroom door at home time. He would say, 'Good afternoon Miss Noakes. May I come in and speak to you?' How could I resist such good manners?

He would then say something like, 'And how was your day today? I particularly enjoyed my Science lesson'. He was one of the few children I have met in a long teaching career who actually knew how to make conversation without being prompted with questions. He was a delight.

John trained and encouraged the two boys in their sporting talents. In the summer term they both took part in all areas of athletics. At that time we had high jump, long jump and throwing competitions, as well as a range of track events. The boys interchanged in first and second places for all these events, so the climax really came on sports day. Which of them was going to win the sprint? I think all the staff were fascinated by their talent and rivalry. Even Miss Perry, still head of the First School, came out onto the field to see the final.

Strange as it might seem, I don't remember who won on that day. It didn't really matter. What did matter, and what I do remember, is that they both shook hands at the end of the race in front of 300 pupils and their parents. They were great role models. There wasn't a glimmer of envy or jealousy between them. The best man won on the day and they both understood this. If only children and sportsmen today could be as gracious.

In that first year after John's arrival it was great, as a youngish teacher, to see the changes that began to take place. So different from the days of Mr Thomas!

As the end of the autumn term approached John mooted the idea of a Fun Morning.

Fun Morning was usually held on the last day of that term, just before the Christmas holidays. It was a bit like a talent competition but there were no prizes. Children were encouraged to perform in front of each other. They could tell jokes, act out little plays, sing, dance or perform in whatever way they wished. It was a bit like 'Britain's got Talent', except that there wasn't a great deal of talent, but it was a great deal of fun. John was the compère. In more recent years he pretended that Sky TV cameras were hidden, filming the occasion. To begin with the children were all amazed and scanned the hall for those hidden cameras. Even as they grew older and realised the joke, they played along with it.

John would begin each Fun Morning with 'The Cuckoo Song' (a clapping song) and we all joined in with great gusto. He would always have a little 'singing toy' which would be part of the event and the younger children just loved it. He would speak to the toy, which would then sing some sort of Christmas carol in reply.

It was amazing to see the range of talent the children produced. Generally, in practices, the boys simply wanted to pretend to shoot each other and the girls wanted to dance to tracks of their favourite singers. As time went on it seemed to me that the children needed more and more help and direction from us, as teachers, to come up with something funny or clever.

I am sure that their imaginations, inventiveness and talent dwindled over the years. Any children who had real talent were embarrassed and didn't want to 'show off' in front of their friends. We worked hard to encourage them, but we were not always successful. At times some were brave enough to play the piano, Indian drums, perform high-class gymnastics and Indian dances, none of which they learned at school. While many of our children attended a wide range of clubs outside school, achieving success in a range of fields - tennis, karate, theatre, song and dance - it was almost impossible to encourage them to show their peers what they had achieved. Sadly the only thing that gained any kudos was success in football or athletics.

The last part of Fun Morning was the staff panto, which, like Fun Morning, became a yearly tradition. But this was completely new to us that first year. I was cast as a witch and John's friend Val provided the costumes and make up. Mick, her husband, accompanied the event on drums. I was duly given a few well-placed warts on my face and judging by the reaction of the children I looked really awful and very scary. John had written the script; he wrote the scripts for all the staff pantos for many years to come. He always interspersed jokes in the scripts which, in rehearsal, he usually had to explain to the staff. The one and only rehearsal would take place after school, usually the day before the performance or, if we were really lucky a couple of days before. It was literally so that we knew where to go on stage. Some of the more diligent staff would actually learn their lines and John, as an actor and the writer, always learned his. I never did. I'd find different ways of secreting the script somehow – in hats, inside a cloak, as part of a prop. Towards the end I wouldn't even try to hide it. The kids didn't care.

Of course there was a lot of typecasting. I was always the evil one who shouted and cackled my way through the script. I did ask John if one year I could play someone nice, but it was not to be. The younger children came to watch, and those pantos were probably the reason I didn't have too much trouble with discipline; they came into the Middle School absolutely terrified of me.

Remember 'Top of the Form' on TV? At the end of the spring term we organised our own version, which was called the 'Interhouse Quiz'. This was to allow the more academic children to have a chance to shine. There were lots of opportunities at school for the pupils to show their talents dramatically, musically and in the many areas of sport; the quiz tested their understanding and knowledge in other areas of the curriculum and tested their general knowledge. Literacy, numeracy, science, history and geography, among other things, formed the basis for the rounds. A quick-fire round at the end often sorted out the placings and also showed how clever some of our children actually were. It was quite impressive and was usually a needle match between the older children, although representatives from all year groups made up the teams.

But it was fun as well, and we tried to include as many pupils as possible. The Middle School children were all allocated a 'house' to which they belonged for the duration of their time with us. In the early days the houses were named after explorers: Wright (blue) after Wilber and Orville, the aviators, Drake (yellow) after Sir Francis, Scott (green) of the Antarctic and Campbell (red) after Donald (although he wasn't an explorer). These names were in place when I arrived at the school. Some time later the school reverted to the four basic colours. A preliminary quiz held in class sorted out the top scorers in each colour. Since the majority of the quiz was oral it did give the children who weren't great at writing a way in, and this proved interesting. Sometimes the most unlikely children had the widest general knowledge.

Apart from subject knowledge, we had a 'Countdown' round where the children were challenged to make the longest word they could from nine random letters. We had video rounds where a short extract was shown to them and questions related to these were asked. Probably the round the staff hated the most was 'Who wants to be a millionaire?' It followed the format of the TV show, except 'Ask the audience' became 'Ask the other children in your colour house'. It often proved useless, since the other children usually had absolutely no idea and simply guessed. For 'Phone a friend' the children were allocated a member of staff who left the hall and was called back if their help was needed. I was responsible for organising this round and took great delight in making the questions more and more difficult as time went by. How cruel was that! At times I was almost bribed to give teachers the answer.

Towards the end of the summer term we would have our Summer Fair, an occasion which always took place on a Saturday and an occasion I grew to hate. I think it was because the children who had left us to go to High School often returned with younger siblings and their families. Sadly the ex-pupils found it an opportunity to try and demonstrate how 'big' they now were by being rude and disrespectful – they knew we had no power over them. Or they would come over and say, 'Hello,

Miss', and then wait for us to make conversation, which was usually followed by monosyllabic answers.

In that summer term of 1981 I decided to be a fortune teller. I dressed appropriately in a gypsy-style long, colourful dress and headscarf. A family had brought their caravan on to the school site, which was where I set up. A sign outside said, 'Fortune Telling. Cross my palm with silver'. I had a very, very basic understanding of palmistry and Tarot cards. Boy, was I popular! In no time at all a hugely long queue began to form. With the Tarot readings it was taking about 15 minutes per person at least and the 'silver' was usually the smallest silver coin they had. I have to say it was the adults who were queuing, not the children! I soon realised this wasn't going to work so I decided to change to palm readings, which should have been quicker. I wasn't prepared for the fact that my 'clients' were taking it all too seriously and I seemed to be hitting the nail on the head. If I said something like, 'I can see in your heart line that you have had quite a few relationships' I received responses like, 'Oh, yes, you are so right but do you think the one I'm in now is the right one?' I then had to listen to a diatribe of woes. I never committed myself to anything. Heck I wasn't a counsellor – I wasn't really a fortune teller. It was exhausting.

At one point during the afternoon I had to have a break. So I said goodbye to the last customer and decided to have a cigarette. Smoking wasn't looked down upon in the same way it is today. The only place to put the ash was on a paper plate, which I placed on the cushions beside me. Someone came and told me that the queue was growing, so I had to let the next person in. I put my ciggie on the paper plate next to me. While

I was reading the next palm I realised I could smell smoke. The cigarette had burned through the paper plate into the cushion. There was no fire and I easily put it out, but there was a big hole in the cushion. I felt so guilty. They were a lovely family who had lent their caravan and I never admitted to the damage and they never said a word. That guilt and shame is still with me and to add insult to injury I made very little money. I never offered my services as a fortune teller again.

Chapter 16

———✄———

The years moved on. I had met Robert in 1980 and we moved into our first house together in 1984. This was a three-bedroomed terraced house in old Southall. It had lovely original features and we ended up staying there for many years until my retirement.

Our neighbours were interesting. On one side we had a Portuguese family. There were six boys and we never heard a peep out of them. On the other side was an Indian family - mum, dad and two very small boys when we moved in. Through the walls we would almost constantly hear mum screaming at the top of her voice at the children. At night time the boys would start crying and it would simply not stop. I think their parents just ignored them. We used to bang on the wall in the hope that mum or dad would do something to quieten them. Some hopes!

As the boys grew up, things became increasingly difficult for us. As teenagers, gangs of their friends would gather in the street outside our house late at night through to the early hours. It was clear that drugs were being sold by the boys from next door. On one occasion the younger brother was shot in the arm outside in the street. We were constantly plagued by noise both inside and outside their house.

Eventually, after several years of hassle, police contacted us. They wanted to search our garden for drugs, and I was amazed one morning when I opened the front door on my way to work to find the police with a battering ram forcing an entry into their house. A detective connected to the drug squad contacted us again and asked if I could meet him, which I did secretly at an arranged time at the local sub police station. I was told that they had found a very small amount of crack cocaine, along with a still which the father had made in a concrete shed at the bottom of their garden. I was asked if I would make a witness statement which would be used in a court case to accuse the family of running a crack house. My name would be withheld. As it turned out it would have been very easy to identify me, since I mentioned my concern for my daughter. I was the only person in the street with a young girl.

The court case was held and the family were duly denied access to their house and metal barricades put on all the windows and doors so that they could not regain entry. This was an incredibly stressful time for me. It coincided with Robert being away. I couldn't sleep and actually had three days off work. I would sit upstairs looking out of the window from behind the curtains and watched events unfold. The family were prevented from returning for three months and it was the quietest Christmas we had ever had.

Chapter 17

Thankfully things were now a little quieter at school, although it did have its moments of tension. I had been teacher rep on the school governing body during the Tommy days. These were crushingly boring occasions which went on forever. I was relieved to hand over the role to someone else and indeed, under Dave I think things improved and became more efficient. A new chairperson, was appointed. She had four children, one boy and three girls, who all went through the school, and she was a fiery character. I didn't like her much at all. To be honest I think I've always had a problem with dominant women. Maybe because they remind me of myself?

The lady was often floating around the school making her presence felt and I think Dave was rather intimidated by her. Anyway a couple of years after she took up this role, Jo Handley and I discovered that she had told Jane, a teacher in the First School that we had said teaching the younger children was easier than teaching the older ones. We had said nothing of the sort. We were furious, and told Dave that we wanted an explanation.

He said, 'Do you want to speak to her?' and we said we did. Oh my word! The following day Jo and I were pulled out of class and asked to wait at the top of the stairs. We were so frightened we were giggling madly, jumping up and down, our hearts pounding. We were summoned in to Dave's office to find her seated there. Dave hovered by the door nervously and then she let rip.

She went ballistic. 'How dare you accuse me? I said no such thing. Who do you think you are?' And so on. We were gobsmacked. I wasn't prepared to back down, but we had to be careful to keep Jane's name out of things although, of course, she knew who had told us. 'If that's what you think of me I will resign!' she screamed. I thought yes, go for it but Jo, who never really liked conflict, tried to calm things down by appeasing her.

'I don't think it's come to that. If you say you didn't make that comment maybe we got it wrong,' she said. I said nothing. I intended to stand my ground. At this point I think Dave suggested we all take time to consider things calmly and Jo and I returned to our classrooms. She didn't resign and she didn't back down.

However, we did nearly make her resign on another occasion. The lady was generally not popular with the staff. We didn't like the initiatives she brought to school. We didn't like the way she implied she knew better than us; the way she swanned around the school, and eventually things came to a head. As a staff, we decided to see if we could bring in a vote of no confidence against her. We had a meeting to which we invited union representatives. I can recall us all sitting in a circle and being asked to list our complaints, which we did, but they were all a little tenuous.

'You can't get rid of someone because you don't like them'

we were told in no uncertain terms by the union reps. There were a few concrete issues, but we were advised that they were not really strong enough. The meeting broke up and she stayed for a while. When she did leave she trained to be a teacher and I hope this gave her a different, more sympathetic view of teaching from the other side.

We had a range of adults who had differing roles within the school over the years – not as class teachers, but who were no doubt as important and as valued by the staff and the children. When I arrived, Barbara Hancock and Grace Newnham worked in the Middle School and Janet, as mentioned, was the secretary. No classroom assistants, no parent helpers.

Barbara was a large lady who had some difficulty walking. Her main role, apart from dealing with sick or injured children, as I recall, was as a tea lady. She would trundle slowly along the corridor with her trolley, providing us with cups of tea in our classrooms during lesson time. We had a domestic science room next to the science room and every afternoon a couple of children from the oldest classes would have the job of washing up the cups. No dishwashers in those days. No sink in the staff room either. Barbara would supervise the children, who would be out of class for at least half an hour a day and who were paid sixpence at the end of the week for their efforts.

Grace was the lady who sorted out the stock. She was a very timid, quiet woman. As teachers, in Tommy's days we each had a little green book into which we would write down the stock we needed for the following week. We had to hand these to Grace every Tuesday morning, first thing. If we were late that was just tough as far as Tommy was concerned. The stock cupboard was always locked, except on that one day of the week.

Grace and Barbara would also accompany the children on day trips. One of these was to Thorpe Park. I remember on one occasion that it was a lovely sunny day and Grace sat on the grass even more quietly than usual. She complained of a headache. That evening at home Grace sadly passed away. I think it was a stroke. We were all very shocked, as you can imagine.

Grace and Barbara were replaced by Jill Brown and Jenny Bashford. Both were lovely ladies, with children of their own. Jenny lived out of catchment, but Jill's three children attended the school. There were twins, Andrew and Laura, and an elder boy whose name was Robert. Robert was in my class one year and we had been looking at astrology, writing made-up forecasts for the signs of the zodiac. I told the children I was born under the sign of Virgo. Jill came into school one morning and said loudly in the staffroom, 'Robert was talking about you last night, Eve. He announced loudly at dinner that you're a virgin'. It was difficult not to laugh out loud!

I said, 'I'm sure I don't know what you're implying.' But everyone in the staffroom chortled heartily about that.

Jenny remained at the school for many years, eventually becoming the school secretary or administrator. She was and still is a bubbly, sociable soul who could always be relied upon to organise flowers, presents, parties and events. Extremely proud of her two children, David and Wendy, she would love to show us photos of them and later of her grandchildren. Jill left after a few years when her husband's job required them to move out of London.

Chris Benson and Pat Bealle were also a twosome but worked mostly in the First School and it wasn't until much later, when the school amalgamated, that I really grew to know them both. Again their children had attended the school and they were both always there at out-of-hours school events. Invaluable at pricing the plethora of second-hand objects at the Blue Peter bring-and-buy sales or at the summer fairs, selling refreshments on a Saturday at the Southall area sports or dressing children for the school productions, they were tireless stalwarts at all sorts of events. They were also greatly loved by the children, for whom they showed equal care and concern with regard to looking after them when they were sick and as teaching assistants working alongside teachers. They showed dedication above and beyond the call of duty. They both decided to leave us in the same year, although Pat returned to run a breakfast club and for many years Chris still came back occasionally to help out.

In the last few years of my teaching things had changed hugely. We had an excellent team of T.A.s who were allocated to certain year groups or classes. This was something I found difficult to become used to. I always arrived very early in the morning and by the time my T.A., Jo Codrington, arrived I had already prepared for the day. Although that might sound great for the T.A., I don't think it necessarily was. I made her feel rather redundant. I had to learn how to make full use of an extra adult in the classroom and I'm not sure I entirely cracked it by the end; I was just too independent.

Another area which took me a while to adapt to was ICT. In 1974 I had a blackboard and chalk. I had a tape recorder to listen to pre-recorded BBC school broadcasts – Singing

Together, Music and Movement, Time and Tune. Later we had an enormous TV on which Chris Benson would record videos. You could then watch them with your class, provided the TV wasn't being used either by another class or for recording other programmes. We didn't have televisions in our rooms.

Of course, the introduction of the computer helped a bit, although floppy discs, which weren't at all floppy, didn't always work. With only one computer and no whiteboard it was fairly useless. A group of four children could just about sit around it.

The old blackboards had to be painted during the summer holidays. Some of them had ruled lines for writing on and some had squares. You could lift the blackboard out of its wooden frame (if you were strong and fit enough) and turn it over so that you were able to use both sides. But really they were a pain and so, when whiteboards were fitted in the classrooms, it was definitely an improvement, although I had to get used to the special pens and on more than one occasion I used a jumbo felt tip by mistake, which of course did not wipe off easily. The use of an overhead projector for which we made transparencies which could be projected onto the whiteboard was a fantastic advance at the time. I continued to use it right to the end. Both young staff and children were fascinated by this 'relic'.

The introduction of interactive whiteboards and the use of the internet changed the face of teaching. With an excess of resources available, teachers can now find an enormous amount of material for any lesson. Heaven help you on those days when the internet was 'down'. I suppose those of us 'oldies' were perhaps better able to cope, since we didn't need to rely on this technology.

We had many staff training sessions to show us how to use all the newly-installed programs on the server and I did try my best. I have to admit I never really understood how to use all the Active Primary applications, but right until the end I would search the internet for useful websites to use with the children. You Tube could be relied upon to have something relevant to the lesson you were teaching.

A computer suite was installed and in the years before I retired I felt we followed an ICT curriculum which was boring and mundane for the modern child, many of whom knew how to use the computer far in advance of what the lessons taught. However, having said that, despite having computers in most homes, some children clearly only used them to play games and even by Year 6 were unable to use a word processing program. A single class of children would provide a huge range of skills.

Chapter 18

For me the 1980s was a fairly quiet decade. I was sort of settled into a relationship with Robert, although we did have moments of doubt and it wasn't plain sailing. However, when you have committed to a mortgage together, it isn't easy to set yourself free.

These were the years when teaching grammar skills became redundant - let the children simply express themselves, they said, they don't need to know about nouns, verbs and adjectives. I was never a believer. I remember naively saying to Dave that I wasn't going to do any more story-writing with the children because what they produced was endless amounts of rubbish. I don't think it occurred to me at the time to teach them *how* to write. I'd give them an idea and expect them to produce something interesting. Quite rightly, he pointed out to me that allowing the children to express themselves in writing was important and, with the introduction of the literacy hour, I began to have an understanding of the best way to teach English. I didn't agree with all the approaches. I hated the snapshots using endless extracts from great children's literature without allowing the children to read the whole book. I hated the time restrictions, ten minutes of this, twenty minutes of that and I never ever got to grips with the plenary. I would much rather recap at the beginning of the next lesson than stop the children in flow at the end of a lesson.

We had used SMP to teach Maths. This was a card system which 'taught' children individually. The children would work through endless cards which tested their understanding of many areas of Maths. Card after card would give them practice in the four areas of arithmetic. The other areas of Maths (algebra, geometry etc) were also on the cards, but with a class of children all working from different cards, it was incredibly difficult to give any teacher input.

In time 'Peak mathematics' was introduced. We were able to teach an area of Maths to the whole class and then follow this up by giving work of appropriate levels and different books to the children. Setting didn't come in until much later, so we were trying to accommodate all abilities. As my understanding of teaching Maths grew, I began to love it and I think my understanding of how to teach effectively eventually resulted in my Year 6 classes achieving to the very best of their ability. The children would often say that they enjoyed their numeracy lessons enormously.

In the 1980s I taught the younger Middle School classes. The school was located beside the Grand Union canal and we considered it important that the children should learn to swim. Sadly there was an occasion when one of the Asian mums had thrown herself into the canal and died. There were times when the canal froze over during the winter and a few of the children attempted to skate on the ice. There was a lock just by the school and, of course, there were idiots who thought it clever to walk across the lock gates. Therefore it was vital that the children should learn how to swim.

This was definitely not a pursuit favoured by the majority of families and some of the children, particularly the girls, were absolutely terrified. From a teaching point of view it was great. Virtually the whole of Tuesday afternoons were taken up with getting on the coach, a twenty-minute swimming session which we didn't teach, and returning to school on the coach.

We went to the local high school for our weekly swimming lessons. There were many children who, after a year, still never got past wearing their armbands. One memory that has never gone away was Marjeline Brown, a girl of West Indian origin. Apparently many West Indian families have a deep seated fear of drowning. How many West Indians achieve Olympic gold medals for swimming? It's just one of those things. Anyway, toward the end of the year the swimming instructors were becoming increasingly frustrated with the lack of progress. Marjeline, amongst others, was told to climb down the steps into the deep end of the pool. She was wearing arm bands and the instructor was in the pool with her. Marjeline panicked and flailed around in the pool. I was standing by the side.

'Come on Marjeline, you'll be absolutely fine. Look, you've got your arm bands on. Just try to swim' I encouraged her.

She looked up at me with tears in her eyes and said, 'My mummy won't like it if I die in the water.' I found it immensely moving, but I have to admit I also found it quite funny. She was in no danger at all and was, of course, absolutely fine, although she never actually mastered swimming while she was with us.

Another fairly humorous incident, this time involving my

health, took place on sports day. Nothing to do with the children. I had had ganglions on both of my wrists for some time. I used to have one on my hand, which was fun to make move up and down. They never hurt and I gathered were just a build-up of fluid or something. Anyway, I was given an appointment at the hospital to have them removed, which happened to coincide with our yearly school sports event. In the morning I duly went off to Ealing Hospital and was fairly horrified by the fact that the surgeon wanted to explain everything and show me what he was doing. I am really squeamish. I once fainted watching 'Your Life in their Hands' on TV. The funniest thing was that I arrived back at school during sports day with two bandaged wrists. There was a buzz amongst the parent spectators and I heard a mum say, 'Oh my god, Miss Noakes has tried to commit suicide. I didn't think teaching was that bad!'

A very exciting event during the eighties was when Michael Rosen, the poet, came to school. As far as I recall the NUT were on strike. I had previously been a member but didn't agree with the way in which, as a member, you could choose whether to strike or not. My opinion was that if your chosen union was fighting for something you should follow and support them. I then joined the NASUWT, a different union, which would only pull out its members when there was no alternative and expected everyone to follow the union advice.

So for about a week and a half many of us went into school but had no children to teach. The few remaining teachers would arrange worksheets for the children, many of whom would arrive at lunchtime to pick up homework and deliver the work they had been set the previous day. For some reason, most of the First School children still came to school as usual. I may have got my facts wrong here, since I am sure many of the First School teachers must have been members of the NUT. Whoever was on strike, the said situation did take place.

Michael Rosen had been booked for the younger children well in advance and, since I had no pupils to teach I was lucky enough to be able to go and see him entertaining the infants. And he was magnificent. Never to be forgotten. His rapport with the children was amazing. He delivered 'Going on a Bear Hunt' brilliantly and we all ended up with huge smiles on our faces. Without that strike I would probably never have seen him.

In later years I was privileged to attend a course run by Pie Corbett, who was and still is a total inspiration. His approach to teaching a huge range of literacy skills was fundamental to my own approach to teaching. The desire and ability to encourage reluctant writers was a revelation. Short, fun challenges, with no sense of failure was the key, while gently attempting to encourage the children to be brave enough to try to achieve more. He gave ideas which would stimulate imagination and courage. Of all the facilitators I have been fortunate enough to have been inspired by, I think that he was probably the best.

I have to say that not all of the courses run by my local authority were worthy of mention, but a few were. I became increasingly interested in Gifted and Talented Children. We were told that on average each school should have 10% of children who could be assessed as such, so I asked the teachers to name the children who they considered should be on the register. I also had questionnaires for their parents and indeed for the children themselves. The teachers generally named the pupils who performed best in tests – often nice, well-behaved little girls. I had forms (scales) for teachers to fill in. One notable section asked about how willing the child was to question and challenge the teacher – a classic sign of the truly gifted child. Most of the children on the teachers' lists came out very poorly on this category.

It was very interesting to attend a course run by Barry Treare. I had used his books in school with the Gifted & Talented children. The more he spoke the more I realised that really, at our school, we had very few children in this category. I taught G&T groups for over 10 years and I think that during this time we probably had fewer than ten children who would truly have deserved to be assessed as such. Amongst many wonderful points Barry had to make, the one thing that stuck in my mind was the child who, when asked in an exam to write about a cricket match, left the page blank. At the bottom of the page he wrote 'Rain stopped play'!

Steve Howkett was another inspiration. Good looking and charismatic, he had some amazingly inventive ways of teaching. These basically focused on literacy using dice and a range of grids to allow the children to arbitrarily make decisions about what they could write about. I went on to use many of his ideas. One of which was 'Jones lay dead on the floor of the room'. By a process of questioning, the children could invent a story of their own. I used a variety of his books throughout my teaching to great effect.

I would like to think that I always attempted to keep my interest in teaching alive throughout the years. During the eighties I was given the opportunity to go on a course which had the title 'Schools in industry and curriculum change'. This essentially gave me the chance to learn about ways in which children at primary school level could begin to understand how the world of work functioned. A part of this was running mini-enterprises with the children. This entailed them working on a range of jobs in order to make money. The children were allowed a certain amount of money and had to make a profit. This was long before 'Dragon's Den'.

The most successful group prepared lunches for the staff. They were delicious, based on a ploughman's lunch with salad and pickle. We would order in advance and the children were released from classes an hour before lunch to prepare the food. They did have an adult to help them. At the end of the week we had enjoyed our lunches, but they hadn't made much profit.

Another group were washing staff cars. They were four boys who generally were a complete pain. I thought this was their best option. They went down to the car park and I showed them what to do. I do seriously think they tried their best. I don't think they deliberately scratched the cars. They simply didn't understand that if you put a sponge down on a gravelly surface it will pick up stones which aren't great on polished metal. When the damage was pointed out to me I had to bring the boys back and their mini-enterprise was finished.

As part of this course I was given the chance to walk around the local council estate with the community policeman, who knew the area well. It was an eye-opening experience. While I had taught these children for some years, I wasn't really aware of where or what they were coming from. Many of their homes were maisonettes above dark, gloomy car parks. There was graffiti and litter everywhere. Large signs declared 'NO BALL GAMES'. There was a shopping parade which apparently was the hub for drug transactions after dark. Teenagers were hanging around street corners when they should have been in school. The whole experience depressed me greatly, but it did help me to understand what our pupils had to cope with: a dull, dirty, uninspiring landscape.

Later that afternoon I went to the main Southall police station, where I had to sign a disclaimer in case anything happened that evening. I was going to be taken out in a squad car around the area. The police driver was a fascinating guy, not one I would say I liked, but he *was* interesting. He was very full of himself, super confident and, I felt, very unnecessarily intimidating in his dealings with the public.

Our first call was to the canal very close to where I lived. A guy had somehow driven his car into the canal. When we arrived, there were already other emergency services there and our services weren't needed. I wasn't allowed to get out of the car (part of the conditions) so I had to rely on sight and feedback from the officers I was with. Apparently the guy driving the car was OK and we soon left the scene.

As it turned out it was a quiet night, incident-wise, so my policeman entertained me with tales of his exploits. He told me that he had become, as the first officer on the scene, a negotiator with a man who was holding a hostage in a flat in Northolt. I remembered this being reported on the news and I didn't doubt that he was telling me the truth. He said he had done an advanced police driving course in which he had to articulate verbally, while driving, everything that he saw in the streets around him. He gave me a demonstration. He kept up an endless description and his observation skills were amazing.

'There's a guy on my left wearing blue jeans, a black leather jacket and trainers. He is carrying a blue and white Tesco bag. A woman on my left has tripped on the pavement. She is in her late fifties. She has a brown raincoat and a brown handbag. A green Ford Escort has just pulled into the road ahead of me. A white Caucasian male is driving and a black female is in the passenger seat.' And so it went on without stopping for about five minutes. He noticed so much more than I did. It was very impressive.

As I've said the evening was quiet, so we began to tour a local council estate which had many ensuing problems. We came across couples and groups of young people strolling around and, as far as I could see, doing no harm. We stopped them and the officer's tone became very aggressive while the people we spoke to were polite and compliant. I didn't like the attitude of my policeman.

Day over and I was delivered back to the police station. It had been a strange experience and convinced me that I would never want to be a policewoman working the streets. You had to be so hard and so tough. I just liked folk too much and would prefer to be pleasant to those people I met. I knew I could never be that hard.

I also spent a week working in an architect's office. I had to arrange this for myself. We had a family whose parents were architects. They were free spirits and the children were interesting. The eldest daughter, Emma, was a confident, determined child. Toby was a little, blonde, amicable boy and Holly, the youngest, was a bit of a loose cannon. Mr and Mrs Fowle were fun-loving creatures. The father was very handsome and she was very pretty. Robert and I frequented the same local pub and we got to know them a little socially, attending the same parties.

Working in the office with them, however, was somewhat disappointing, albeit relaxing. I was given the task of copying architectural designs and so I sat at my desk for a week and did just that. I think I did it well. I wasn't taken out of the office and I wasn't given any access to the way their business worked, but it fulfilled the requirements of the course.

I never finished that course. I didn't complete all the paperwork, which was typical of me. But it had been a fantastic experience.

Chapter 19

By 1987 I needed something to spice up my life again. I mentioned this to Robert and he was happy for me to go off and have an adventure. I'd been at college with Angela Gwatkin, whom we had all called Rosie, her middle name, since there were two Angelas. I had kept in touch with Rosie over the years. She had left teaching to run her own catering business. She lived in Highgate, had a lovely flat, was unattached and, like me, fancied doing something different.

We decided to go to Thailand and Burma during my summer holidays. We did a great deal of research and used a travel company (Trailfinders) to help us plan and arrange our tour. We were going to be backpackers, which was quite adventurous since we were both in our mid-thirties. We planned to be away for four weeks, one of which would be spent in Burma.

I kept a diary throughout my visit. We flew out on 26th July to Bangkok on Kuwaiti airlines, which was an experience in itself and not a particularly good one. We had a long stopover in Kuwait, where we had to remain in a cold inhospitable airport for hours while cockroaches crawled around our feet in the toilets. However, we arrived in one piece and found a cheap place to stay. My diary described my impressions on arrival:

We have now found ourselves a fairly poor but decent abode, The Dior Guest house in Khao San Road, close to the Golden Palace. A small room with two beds, communal shower and toilets close by. This whole area is overrun with tourists doing it on the cheap and they equal the natives in profusion. BUT there is that essence of Bangkok. The joyous, playful laughter of the Thai girls, holding hands as they walk down the road. The insanity and carbon monoxide poisoning of the traffic. Complete recklessness of the motor cyclists. Deformed dogs allowed to live in agony. In this Buddhist country no one kills animals even if it is to put them out of their misery! Little old ladies laden down with yolks like the milkmaids of bygone days. Heat, constant sweat. Incredibly heavy, painful rucksacks, the straps digging in to your shoulders. Total pleasure at being here and total exhaustion. Time to go to bed.

We spent five days in Bangkok on this occasion and did all the touristy things. On the Thursday we flew on Thai Air to Rangoon in Burma, a fabulous flight. Fantastic treatment from beautiful Thai hostesses. We were soon in for a major culture shock.

I wrote:

Total hassle and bureaucracy from the time you step off the plane until the time you get out of the airport. There are about five different places you must take your passport to and the system is totally inadequate and boss eyed. Passports to be dealt with are piled on top of each other so that if you were first you ended up last. Everyone tries to keep their temper despite the exasperation.

The country is run by the militia and it is quite frightening to have such a strong presence of guns and rifles around.

We had been told that any travel around Burma had to be done legitimately. Train and bus tickets would have to be shown to the authorities when we arrived back at the airport to leave and we could be in deep trouble if we were found to have done anything illegal. I didn't fancy spending years in a Burmese gaol. So what happened next meant that we were very brave or very stupid.

My diary continued:

Eventually we were through and changed our money. Met up with Nicky and Laura, two American girls, for our taxi ride into Rangoon. Taxi rank was amazing. Full of dilapidated Jeeps and cars. On our ride into Rangoon a guy jumped into the Jeep. He offered to drive us around Burma for a certain amount of money from each of us. We met up with an English guy called Nick, who the American girls knew, at the Tourist Burma offices and told him the details. He went off to see the guy around a street corner - all very secretive. Nick returned and we all sat and debated whether we should do it. We decided that we should. (We were later to find that this was really the only way to see Burma properly.)

We were taken to a restaurant on the outskirts of Rangoon. There were going to be three 'guides'. While we ate, two of them went off to get petrol. We wondered whether they would return, although at that point no money had exchanged hands. The guys, Tomtom and Yusuf, did return and we set off at about 10pm. We were asked to keep a low profile as we drove through Rangoon. We got through the checkpoint with ease or should I say with a bribe (paid by the driver) and drove off into the darkness, all of us, I'm sure, feeling a little apprehensive as to what we were letting ourselves in for.

I absolutely loved Burma and the Burmese people we met. There was a refreshing innocence about them. They weren't used to tourists and were delightfully charming, very interested in us while living a very simple, poor lifestyle.

Our guides were fantastic as it turned out, thankfully. We went where they took us and they arranged it all - hotels, restaurants, sightseeing, everything. Imagine being in places with magical names like Mandalay, travelling on a boat up the Irrawaddy. Brilliant!

I think the most memorable thing we did was visiting a hill tribe. It was a long day but unforgettable.

My diary continued:

Rising at twenty past four, while being a shock to the system, was not as bad as I had imagined. I showered in cold water which aided the waking up process and Rosie and I dressed, packed our rucksacks and went downstairs at five to await the arrival of Paul, our guide for the day. Paul was a very quietly-spoken, gentle man who spoke a vast collection of languages: Tamil, Hindu, English, French and many dialects of the tribal people in Burma. He badly wanted to go and live in America and become a pastry cook!

We set off cross country at a cracking pace. We climbed up and up into the mountain side - very hard going. As we went along quite a few of the villagers from the tribe passed us on the way into Kalaw for market day. They carried their produce in big baskets on their backs with all the weight taken on their foreheads by a strap which was attached to the basket. Even young children carried their bags in the same way. They wore tribal clothes, reds, greens and orange woven skirts and boleros. We sampled their bananas which were good and we were told they were also carrying cheroot leaves and other vegetables to market.

Still we travelled further on; with breathtaking scenery below us until after about two hours and seven miles we began to approach the village. We walked along a pathway, walked past their monastery and entered the long house – a long, wooden building raised on stilts, beneath which lived the animals (mostly pigs) squelching about in mud and filth. Apparently the villagers allowed their poo to drop from the long house down to the animals below who ate it.

As we entered the long house we were greeted by the children of the Palaung tribe - grubby little creatures with huge eyes. We were invited to sit down with an elderly man, (not the head man, who had gone into town). The long house was home to 15 families and was divided up into compartments with wooden divisions placed lengthwise but with no partition to the middle, so that each space was open to public scrutiny. There were two completely closed-off areas which we were told were for the use of newly married couples. The house was entirely made of wood and was very dark with only a few window spaces of which one had glass in it.

There was a fire near to the entrance which had been created by lighting wood on a stone base. All of the cooking for the entire house was done here. The fire puffed out black smoke which hung in the atmosphere of the entire hut as there was no chimney through which the smoke could escape. We were shown the 'kiln' where the cheroot leaves were dried in bundles on hot plates above an enormous oven. There was also a certain amount of opium smoking amongst the men.

We sat down to drink tea and eat very dry, roasted, unpalatable sweetcorn and the children, of whom there were many, came to watch us. They were very dirty and barely wore any clothes. Each family had an average of ten children and we were told that very few died in infancy, although some of them appeared to be very malnourished with distended stomachs and thin little arms and legs, runny noses and weeping eyes. One mother was breast feeding another mother's baby as its own mother was ill and there was a tiny little baby, only ten days old, in the arms of a young girl who looked much younger than the 17 years we were told she was. At one point the school teacher, dressed in a huge green lungi, came to collect the children from the hut to go to school. She was a young woman from the local town, Kalaw, who lived in the village while she taught the children. The children attended the school from the ages of 6 to 10 and then some went on to the High School in Kalaw but none had ever gone on further to University.

The Palaung tribe was almost totally self-sufficient, growing all their own foodstuffs. The money they made from selling their produce at market they used to buy wool to weave the material for their clothes, oil for cooking and, in recent times, they had begun to purchase tape machines and cassettes! The community was almost entirely agrarian, growing crops such as tobacco, bananas, rice, corn, carrots, aubergines, squash, tomatoes, beans and other fruit. They bred pigs and slaughtered them for their meat. People would visit the tribe to buy pigs directly from them. There were also chickens and cattle. The rice for the year was stored in a huge vat.

There were three long houses and the one we went in was the largest but some members of the tribe were allowed to live separately in their own houses. Even in the remotest part of Burma in 1987 things were changing. In some tribes, although not this one, the women still wore rings to extend their necks, and rings on their arms and legs. More and more women were refusing to allow this to happen to them.

Our visit was at an end. We gave the teacher some pencils and rubbers and made our way back to the hotel. It had been a completely different world from any I had previously experienced.

We returned to Bangkok for a couple of days before heading north to Chiang Mai after our week in Burma. Our departure from Burma had been terrifying, as we had no way to account for the money we had spent. Rosie and I felt we were in the film 'Midnight Express', our illicit adventures about to be discovered at any time. Our hearts were thumping loudly as we stood in the customs queue. As it transpired we need not have worried. We were asked no questions and passed safely through.

Rosie had an English friend who lived in Songla on the

border of Thailand and Malaysia with whom we spent a pleasant few days. It was great to be back in civilised company. We were taken out for conventional meals, went swimming and it gave us a chance to relax.

For our final week we decided to go to Koh Samui. Once we walked off the ferry we hired a Jeep to Lamui beach. It was awful, dirty and crammed with 'bungalows'. The hippy community still survived there, if nowhere else.

I wrote:

Some very stoned people here. We're sitting in a grotty little eating place which had next to nothing on the menu and I'm pissed off. The whole complex is like Butlin's holiday camp without the children. It is really awful here. The first room we were shown was dreadful, filthy mattress, mosquitoes and it stank. We managed to upgrade slightly but it was still bad. The place appears to be owned by a very garrulous Thai. And it's very hard to understand what he is saying. We were offered dope cookies and I was awake for most of the night as a result imagining all sorts of weird things. I had thought before I went to sleep that it wasn't having any effect!

I hated the place, so Rosie and I set off to find out if there was somewhere better. I continued:

And that's exactly what we did. We have found Paradise at last. A beautifully quiet beach, white sands with waves gently lapping on the shore and hardly a soul in sight.

 It was expensive, compared to any of the other places we had stayed in, but it was worth it. We stayed there for nearly a week during which time the weather was dreadful, which was a shame. It would have been nice to swim and sun bathe but the seclusion made up for it.

We briefly returned to Bangkok and then caught our flight home. Thailand had been a very different experience from Burma. I wrote about Thailand:

Thailand is a strange country, or maybe I'm surprised by my reaction to it. I have felt neither entranced nor disgusted by it. It hasn't really been able to inspire strong enough feelings in me one way or the other - not in the way Burma did. It is very beautiful in parts and almost equally as poor as Burma. However, it has become almost blasé, at ease with the tourists, just a little too sophisticated, not in lifestyle but in attitude. Well, I don't know if I should have expected anything different. Burma definitely spoiled me.

Chapter 20

Back in England, the new school year began. 'Baker Days' or teacher training days had been introduced by the Government, so we had a fairly relaxing start to the year. My birthday is in September and that year I held a party in a restaurant in Ealing. Tess Morgan, who became my best friend, had split up from her husband the previous summer and she was very keen to meet Paul, who was a friend of Robert's and had been my flat mate when I lived above the butchers. I am happy to say that they were both attracted to each other and began what turned out to a long relationship, which only ended when Tess sadly died in 2009.

In 1989 I was eventually rewarded for all my hard work. I applied for and was given an 'A' allowance for Humanities, Equal Opportunities and Community Involvement. It had taken 15 years of total dedication to reach this point.

I was aware that if you stayed at the same school, progress up the ladder was difficult. Many teachers had left us to go on to great things. However, I lacked ambition and considered it more important that I was teaching in a school where I liked the staff and children.

In the January of 1989 Jo had joined the staff. She had been teaching at another school in Ealing where she had begun a relationship with Neil, who also taught in the school. They thought it would be better if they didn't teach together. A sensible decision. I recall Jo arriving for her interview. I liked her instantly. She seemed a little vulnerable but very enthusiastic, and I was delighted when she was offered the post.

Strangely, the way things often happen, a 'B' post became available at the school the following March. I applied to be in charge of 'Inset and Curriculum Planning'. Odd really, since something I always resented about teaching was the written requirements of curriculum planning. I absolutely loved spending my Sundays planning the following week in my head, but I had a 'thing' about committing myself to paper.

During the 1980s Robert and I had experienced many sticky patches, but by the end of the decade we were getting on well. Robert had made it clear to me from the time that we met that he didn't want children, so it came as a complete shock when I discovered that I was pregnant. I had achieved two 'Bs' within two months.

It was difficult telling Robert. I was determined that I would have this baby on my own if I had to. He took the news reasonably well although, of course, it was an enormous shock. I had an amniocentesis to check for abnormalities – I think I would have terminated the pregnancy if it had shown any – but fortunately everything was fine. I found out that the baby was a girl. Robert didn't want to know the sex of the baby and I didn't tell him.

She was due to be born in November. I spent a relaxing

summer holiday not doing much and returned to school in September. This year I had Year 3 children. I made an appointment for a routine check-up at the doctor's on the Friday of the first week back and he told me that he didn't think the baby was growing well enough. I hadn't put enough weight on. He told me to rest for two weeks. Dave brought in a supply teacher, but I didn't really want the class disturbed by me coming and going all the time. So when I returned to the doctor he agreed to sign me off for the rest of my pregnancy. In those days you received sick pay, so I didn't suffer financially.

Kate was born on 24th November and I hadn't worked since July! She was a good healthy size and was gorgeous with lots of black hair. There were plenty of difficult times during the first few months. I remember that on New Year's Eve she wouldn't stop crying, no matter what I did, and I considered putting her in a box and taking her back to Queen Charlotte's hospital! I just couldn't relax. When she slept I worried about what I would do when she woke up. I had no relatives close by and my friends had either had children years ago and returned to work or were younger than me and didn't yet have a family. I had no one to talk to and Robert wasn't handling things well, so that even when he came home from work he would sit in another room, leaving me with Kate. I would often take her to Northampton, but my mum was nearly 70 and too old to look after her for me. On one occasion I drove back home from Northampton and Robert looked at Kate with such venom that I instantly bundled her up and drove to my brother and sister-in-laws in Chertsey.

I couldn't wait to get back to work, but Kate was still breast feeding and waking me several times during the night. I couldn't work if I was exhausted, so I decided I had to do something. About a week before I was due to return in June I put Kate in her cot and got my headphones. When she awoke and started crying I went in, laid her down and went back to my CD player. I could still hear her over the music and I was in pieces, but determined. I must have gone in about four times before gradually the crying lessened. I eventually went in about two hours after she had first started crying and she was lying in a heap, still sobbing in her sleep. I covered her up and went to bed. The following evening I only had to go in once to tell her to go to sleep and after that she slept through the night. Success!

With only six weeks of term left I was asked to take several different classes (which I had always hated) but actually it was fine and gave me a chance to get to know far more children. My little Year 3 class hadn't seen me for months but still thought of me as their teacher - sweet. Kate was being looked after by a childminder, Connie, who I had met through the NCT and who had two small children of her own. I would drop her off at eight in the morning and pick her up when I finished work. This arrangement worked well for a while.

Chapter 21

I was thin, very thin, by the time I returned in September to take a year 5 class. One of the girls in my class said, 'Gosh, Miss Noakes, you've lost a lot of weight. Are you all right?' I had indeed been amazed when I went to buy a pair of jeans to find that I fitted into a size 10 for the first time in my life.

I was all right, just about, and being back in teaching I have to be honest; without having to constantly worry about Kate and Robert, my life began to return to normal. That isn't to say that the continual feeling of fatigue left me. It must have taken about 18 months until I regained some sense of normality.

The 1990s at school were a time of relocation and reorganisation. In 1992 a gradual influx of people from crisis-torn Somalia began to filter into our school. I had one of the first refugees in my class, a lovely, quiet, calm boy called Ahmed. I had never seen people from Somalia before and I was amazed by both his height and his high forehead.

Gradually, as more and more Somali people arrived, we, as teachers, were given help in after-school courses to understand the circumstances from which these children came so that we might better understand them. Nimo, a Somalian girl, entered my class a couple of years later. She was an aggressive, troubled child who had witnessed the deaths of both her father and brother. It took some time for her to accept life in her new country, unsurprisingly.

Possibly the British weather didn't help. In the autumn term of 1995 it rained a lot. Our school had a flat roof and you could hear the rain pouring down the internal drain pipes in the classrooms. However, it was something of a shock when water began to gush into the upper school hall one day at the end of assembly. It came in gallons and gallons. There was absolute panic with the teachers and some of the older children trying to clear it up, but their efforts were futile. The fire brigade was called and eventually things were cleared up, but the borough architects deemed that the school roof desperately needed repair.

As a result the entire school had to relocate! Fortunately an abandoned high school was found for us all to move to while repair work was carried out. Christmas came early as the children were given three days' extra holiday while the staff packed up everything into crates, which a removal firm transported to our temporary home. At the start of the spring term we again had three days to rearrange everything at the other end before the pupils returned.

Strange as it may seem, it was a fun time for us. Yes, the packing was a bit of a pain, labelling the crates and sorting things out at both ends, but it was also exciting and challenging and, of course, for a time we didn't have the children around, so in a way it was a bit of an extra holiday for us too.

I had a fabulously huge classroom at the new site. It was tucked round a corner on the top floor. The only disadvantage was that it was a considerable walk to the staffroom. Playtimes were announced by a pre-set bell system, so timings were rigid. Often I only managed to reach the staffroom as the bell rang for the end of the break.

The new school was closer to where I lived, so I could walk there. Kate had started in Reception that school year and we were able to walk together on occasions. However, I arrived at school far too early for Kate to be hanging around so she went to her brilliant childminder, Peggy, before school and often afterwards. She would then catch the coaches along with the other children which bussed the pupils from Three Bridges to our new site.

As a result, the children usually arrived at about 9.15 and often later, depending on traffic and in the afternoon left our classrooms at 2.45 to get ready for the coach back. Our school days were very much shorter. Not all the pupils caught the buses and they were at school for the normal length of time, but teaching early mornings and late afternoons was virtually impossible with children arriving and leaving at different times.

As staff we had a hoot. The adventure somehow bonded us together even more. Gill Last had left the previous summer and Beattie Earl had replaced her as the Special Needs Co-ordinator. Beattie was great fun and made all of us laugh a lot. Many of us, of all shapes and sizes, started meeting in the staffroom once a week after school to do keep-fit exercises, much to Dave's embarrassment. He walked in on us once and didn't know where to put his face.

Our school was duly repaired and we moved lock, stock and barrel back again. It was good to be 'home' but it had been an interesting experience. Everyone had worked hard to make a difficult situation better, not least the caretaker, who was constantly on call to deal with the contractors at all hours.

Rob Seymore was the site supervisor at the time. I'd always liked Rob and got on well with him, although he didn't always respond particularly promptly to calls of duty. 'My clock's stopped, Rob, Could you fix the kids' coat pegs? My blackboard could do with repainting. None of the lights are working in my classroom, Rob.'

Usually he got round to things, often in his own time. When he first joined us Rob was more than willing to help out at a range of extra-curricular events. He helped erect stage lights for John's productions and took an active part in the Christmas staff panto. He'd join us for social events and was an intelligent, vibrant sort of guy. Sadly as the years passed he had his own demons to tackle, but I was perhaps one of the few members of staff who continued to try to help and support him.

When I had started teaching, Mr Meaburn had been the caretaker. He had two girls who attended the school and both were bright, lively, pleasant little girls who enjoyed gymnastics. He left the school for another job outside London and his assistant, Margaret Gumbleton, took over for a while. She was lovely. In her fifties, I think, and she was a kind, approachable lady. When Robert and I moved into our first house together she gave us a settee. I always remember that she told me she had lost four stone in weight by eating raw onions with every meal! I never tried it myself, but who knows?

Another memorable character was a West Indian guy called Ben. He was also lovely and had an extended family he thought the world of. But Ben often smelt of alcohol when I arrived for work. He was able to carry out his duties well enough. He wasn't with us for long, since he worked on a temporary basis, and it was a shock when I learnt that he had died.

We had a lot of caretakers who spent short times with us, more recently a Polish guy who was also great. We talked about his life in Poland and I admired him a lot for his desire to begin a new life in a new country.

During Rob's time as caretaker, he had sort-of mentored one of my ex pupils, Wayne, who had been in my class when he was about nine. A bit of a wimp at the time (I'm sure he wouldn't mind me saying that), Wayne had gone a little astray at high school. Rob nurtured him and Wayne never really forgot his years at our school.

When Rob eventually left the school we were all highly delighted that Wayne was given his job. A nicer, more positive influence would have been hard to find. Wayne is still always there to help and support his old school in every possible way. An absolute diamond! He is married to Tracy, who works in the canteen and was also taught by me, and is a stepfather to Tracy's two children, Leanne and Sarah. They have a little boy of their own, Craig, and are bringing him up with the same manners and respect they themselves have always shown.

Chapter 22

Ealing primary schools often lost pupils to Hounslow schools at the age of 11, since Hounslow had sixth forms, whereas Ealing high schools finished at the age of 16. Also, with the introduction of the national curriculum, Key Stage 3 began at 11, so middle schools were attempting to teach two stages of education.

Therefore, reorganisation was required, and this took place in 1993. Many first and middle schools were amalgamated as single primary schools. We were, of course, no exception. The implications were one head teacher, one deputy head and fewer posts of responsibility. We had to apply for our new jobs and we were re-interviewed.

Chris Hill, the head of the First School, moved to a larger primary school in Hounslow and Dave Price became head of our new school. Ann Gill had been deputy of the First School for some time. She was a very popular, jolly lady, greatly loved by the children and very supportive to staff, newly qualified or well established, and always happy to join in the spirit of the school.

John Maxwell, of course, I knew better as I had worked closely with him for many years and his charisma and enthusiasm were always evident. It is strange that as two schools on the same site, the two separate groups of staff hardly knew each other. I would walk down the path every morning, enter the premises, turn right and climb the stairs into the Middle School. We had separate staff rooms and separate lives so joining us together was going to be a big challenge for all of us.

Both Ann and John applied for the deputy headship of the 'new' school and John was appointed, which I don't think came as a surprise to Ann, who accepted his appointment with grace. So now all the other posts were up for grabs. Personally I had found life very difficult since Kate was born and I was aware that I was unable to carry out the duties of someone on a B post. Having a baby, though I loved her enormously, is hard when you are 40 and trying to hold down a full-time job.

Before reorganisation I had spoken to Dave and asked if I could relinquish my post, since I thought it unfair to the other staff. I was being paid a higher wage without being able to produce the goods. He was very kind. He told me to wait and give myself some time to try to come to terms with my situation.

With reorganisation I had the chance to apply for a lower level post, which I did. I was offered an A post which I happily accepted. The rest of the posts were allocated, a classroom changed into a joint staffroom and we began the following year as one school.

One member of the First School staff who I was wary of was Miss Heyreh, an Asian teacher who had been at the school longer than I had. I thought she was a bit scary and I wasn't sure how to react to her. But she was a revelation. Very amusing with a sharp droll wit, she didn't suffer fools gladly. It would be true to say that she did indeed scare some of the children and could be quite irascible, but I enjoyed her company immensely. She was rather old-fashioned in her teaching methods and had found it challenging to keep up with new educational initiatives which the government bombarded us with at the time. I was saddened when she retired. I moved into her classroom and she bequeathed me a host of handmade teaching resources, which I kept for a couple of years in case she ever wanted them back. She also left me a wide range of interesting plants which she had tended and watered regularly. Now, I'm afraid my fingers are not green and without the aid of my delightful cleaner, Mrs Dawood, they would have died long before they actually did. Sorry, Joginder.

We settled into our new arrangement. I had changed my name to Mrs Osborne since I considered it easier for Kate, who would soon enter the Reception class. Some teachers moved across the key stages and others remained where they were. I found the new Year 3 (7 to 8-year-old children) challenging and slightly annoying and would not have enjoyed teaching even younger children. I simply didn't have the patience.

Ofsted! Every teacher's nightmare? Well it was certainly mine. I know there are some strange people who relish a group of interlopers entering their place of work, criticising them and, after a snapshot of their work, appraising what they felt about how well they thought you did. But not me.

Our first Ofsted was in 1998 under Dave's headship. We'd had at least four months' notice and had spent weekends at school prior to the visit sprucing the place up. We didn't really know what to expect. I recall that John was very positive and upbeat about it all, at least on the surface, trying to instil confidence in us all.

The 'team' duly arrived, about six of them I think, and introduced themselves to us. They were accommodated in a hut in the playground, where no doubt they discussed us at length without being heard. Everything began quite positively, as I recall. At close of play at the end of the first day we were doing well enough, Dave informed us. And then it went downhill really from that point.

Joginder and I received the most visits. Both of us had twelve of our lessons observed during the course of about three and a half days! It seemed as if one or the other of the team was with me virtually all the time.

I'm sure that I didn't help matters when, after one of the inspectors watched a maths lessons, she asked to see my planning file.

'Um, I don't have one,' I replied. Well, writing it all down didn't mean you were a better teacher in my mind. Mental planning and making resources for the lessons were far more important. The lesson had been good enough, but it was clear that she wasn't impressed. Well, in my own defence, I knew what I was teaching, what I had previously taught, the level of understanding of each individual child and what I expected them to achieve, but I couldn't back that up with written evidence. Evidence was essential. Such was the state of education at that time, and it has been so ever since.

At the end of the inspection we each received our feedback. When I glanced down the page of written grades for the lesson observations, each lesson was itemised and next to each was the word 'Good'.

I recall saying to the inspector, 'What do I have to do to be outstanding?' He didn't reply to that question but said, 'You should be satisfied with your result.'

It was clear as the week went on that something was wrong. I wasn't a member of the management team, so I wasn't privy to what the problems were, but it was obvious that Dave was worried. He made the staff aware that there were difficulties and, in a meeting with staff at the end of the day, he strongly encouraged us to do our very best the following day, which of course we did because we cared about the children, the school and especially Dave.

Annie Thain was teaching a Year 4 class at the time. Annie was a large, eccentric twitcher. I mean that in the best possible way. She was obsessed with bird watching and went on to have fabulous holidays in Peru and many other parts of the world, after which she hosted assemblies showing the wonderful pictures she had taken, talking animatedly about the wildlife she had seen.

She was, as I've just said, eccentric. Possibly then in her early 30s, she was forever experimenting with new ideas in her classroom. I remember at one point that, because the children were too chatty, she turned all the desks so that they faced the walls of the classroom. She did mean well, worked very hard and instigated lots of interesting hands - on ways of teaching science. Her legacy remains at school in terms of worksheets and visual aids.

But this Ofsted was one step beyond for Annie. I've no idea as to the details of what happened, but apparently the pressure for her was such that she left her class and her classroom during an inspection lesson and ended up sitting on the canal bank beside the school while she composed herself. Clearly very odd behaviour, which probably didn't help our cause.

I think we escaped Special Measures by the skin of our teeth and we all let out a sigh of relief when the inspectors eventually left on Friday. One of my most abiding memories during that week was that it had been full of completely mixed emotions; one minute we were up and elated, the next down and desperate. Another memory that remains clearly in my mind was, even after we knew things weren't great, seeing John 'calmly' tidying the library, sticking labels on books early in the morning as if life was just dandy. What was that about? Maybe it was his way of dealing with things.

We had just about got through and it was a bit of a shock for all of us. Perhaps it was time to sharpen up our act.

Chapter 23

———— ✄ ————

Dave decided to retire in 2002. He had endured long journeys every day to and from his home in Oxfordshire and came to the conclusion that it was his time to leave. He had inherited a school that was stuck in the past and had brought it into the 21st century. Dave had established a relationship of respect with the staff, the children and the parents of the school.

I had had my moments with Dave. On one memorable occasion we were having a meeting at his house when he mentioned some concerns about a particular girl. I resented the fact that he had not told me about a child who was at risk in my class (apparently it was not thought, at the time, that class teachers should be privy to such information). I used to call it the SS. How were we supposed to understand if we didn't know?

We were both smokers and often, amongst outcasts, there is a chance to chat perhaps more openly when they are outside in the freezing cold. We often talked about our families and in Dave's final year as head, Kate had reached Year 6. I had specifically asked him not to place me as a teacher with her year group and I was furious when he told me that I would in fact be teaching Year 6. She wouldn't be in my class, but I had known these children for seven years and thought it might be difficult both for her and for me. But, to be fair, he didn't really have much choice. Kate's class had been messed around in Year 5. Her teacher had left on maternity leave and her replacement had difficulty controlling the class. Dave wanted some stability for the year group. Kate was to be in John's class and I was to take the parallel class. They weren't an easy bunch, but it turned out fine in the end.

And so interviews were held to replace Dave and we were all on tenterhooks, trying to catch a glimpse of the candidates.

'Oh, I didn't like the look of her,' Jo remarked as one of the candidates strode purposely down the corridor.

'And did you see him? He looks scary,' I commented.

As the day of the interview progressed the candidates were whittled down. Beattie took me into her room to introduce me to Matt Burdett, a young, handsome man, and I was instantly impressed. Of course I had no idea how good he might be at the job, but he was very personable and a bit of eye candy in charge of a virtually female staff would have been nice.

As things turned out, Matt was given the job. It was his first application for a headship and I think a bit of a surprise for him. Another inexperienced head that we could mould and manipulate, we thought. Not at all!

As Dave's retirement became imminent (I'm talking about the day before) he suddenly became ill. A stomach upset. On his final day we had a leaving assembly arranged and his 'do' in the evening for staff and friends. Getting him on to the stage to say goodbye to the children was a close thing. He made it as brief as possible, but he managed. Dave was then collected by his wife,

Chris, and taken home. None of us knew whether he'd be able to make it back for the evening.

But he did. Looking very pale, he managed to deliver a lovely speech and then the dancing began. Within about 30 minutes Dave was bopping with the rest of us. Having got over the whole ordeal, he was able to relax and start enjoying himself. There were no signs of his previous discomfort, and I completely understood. Those of us who suffer from nerves and anxiety in certain situations would have totally sympathised with him. It is only after the pressure drops that you can start to enjoy everything. It was a great evening and a fitting goodbye to Dave.

There were three more visits from the Ofsted inspectors during my time at the school, in 2003, 2007 and during my final year, 2011. I have little recollection of the first two of these experiences. Suffice it to say they were considerably more low key than the horrible first occasion. Matt had very recently taken up the headship in 2003 and was really beginning to make his mark on the school, which I'm sure was taken into consideration by the team. All I can recall is that my music lesson was observed. Now I can't sing in tune and I have absolutely no knowledge of playing any instruments, so I was very rash in timetabling a music lesson for the period of time the inspectors were on site. I think most teachers placed it on days when Ofsted weren't there. It was no surprise at all when the inspector walked into the classroom. My lesson was based on looking at artworks and then asking the class to compose music using a range of untuned instruments to match the images. My abiding memory was of her saying as she left the room, 'You were very brave!' I'm sure she knew I didn't have a clue.

The inspection in 2007 is a complete blur and I recall nothing of note, but the school was doing well. The report said, 'This is a good and improving school'.

I certainly won't forget my final Ofsted. From the outset the inspectors were very pleasant and approachable. What a difference from the first time! I was only observed once, during a literacy lesson. We were following up from a production of Oscar Wilde's 'The Happy Prince' which we had seen the previous day when a theatre group had visited school. The theme of my lesson was the correct use of question marks following a well-written sentence. I gave the children the answers and their task was to compose suitable questions, which they all did extremely well, each child at their own level producing some excellent work.

The inspector was very impressed and commented that my lesson was outstanding. So after 36 years I had made it at last! My elation was somewhat tempered when teachers in their first and second years of teaching also achieved outstanding results, but clearly Matt had chosen his staff well and I was, of course, very happy for us all. The school as a whole was also deemed outstanding at the end of the visit and we were all justifiably proud of ourselves.

And so all good things must come to an end. As John was nearing his 60th birthday during the next academic year, he decided it was time to retire from the job he had dedicated his life to. With a great many interests outside school, his freedom would allow him the chance to pursue his love of travel, the theatre, music and reading when and where he wished. He duly tendered his notice early in the autumn term so that Matt and the governing body would have ample time to interview for a replacement and prepare for his departure. Ever the considerate gentleman!

John was a huge part of our school and clearly deserved the very best of a combined retirement and birthday party. Jo and I, amongst others, were not going to allow him to leave without a fuss. Besides John, the showman, would have been disappointed with anything less than a grand event.

The party, of course, took place at school with the hall decorated in the school colours of blue and yellow – John's choice. Both friends and colleagues were invited and the staff sang and danced for him. Admittedly we gave a rather pathetic rendition of a Popmobility routine and there were comic routines by Jo and myself on video based on the fact that we were always gossiping about one thing or another but never in a cruel way, I hasten to add. John was sort of forced into singing the Cuckoo Song which had started every fun morning since time began, and Matt referred to the Sky TV cameras which were filming the event. The entire hall joined in with great enthusiasm, whether they knew the song or not.

Ken Woolcott, the founder of Popmo and John's very close friend, composed and recited a humorous poem and both Matt and Dave spoke eloquently of the amazing contribution John had made throughout the years and of the legacy of traditions which he would leave behind and of the ambition he inspired in the children.

The evening was a truly joyous event full of fun and humour and was greatly enjoyed by all. It was our chance to say thank you to a true professional.

To this day John continues to play an active part in the life of the school several years after his retirement by leading song practices, continuing to produce and direct plays and supporting and training the children in a wide range of sporting events. He ensures that his legacy does indeed live on.

Chapter 24

I wasn't far behind John in terms of age, but perhaps my own enthusiasm waned far more than his ever did. In my last few years of teaching I did continue to take every opportunity to try new ways in which to interest and enthuse my students. One example was through the Creative Partnership, an initiative that linked schools to a range of creative practitioners, mostly through the arts. We were lucky enough to welcome artists, actors and storytellers amongst others, who worked with the children to produce some brilliant results.

I was fortunate enough to work with my Year 5 class on creative grammar, which was a visual stimulus to help children understand and become more familiar with grammar and employ a range of grammar correctly in their writing. Following weekly focused lessons the children went on to produce fantastic stories which they were then shown how to animate on computers. One of my pupils, Vivek, was a whiz in the computer room and he was really my mentor. Two Irish guys taught the children how to animate the stories they had written and when they left, whatever I had forgotten, Vivek remembered.

Notably one of the pupils in my class, Steven Sharp, who was on the autistic spectrum and had difficulty coping with the requirements of academic learning, responded extremely well to these sessions, retaining information and applying what he had learnt to his own writing. It was quite remarkable.

The creator of this system, Teresa, was married to Andrew, who worked for Sky TV. He arranged for a camera crew to come to school to film the children working on their stories. All very exciting! We were then invited to Sky where further scenes for a DVD were filmed. Julie Etchingham was the anchorwoman and I found the whole process fascinating. The children, of course, took it all in their stride. As long as food was provided they were happy.

We were given a tour of the newsroom, where I bumped into Francis, whom I had last seen almost thirty years before. He was in the weather room and I said, 'Remember me?'

'Of course', he replied, although I'm not sure if he could remember my name. We arranged to meet for a drink at the pub which had been our local all those years ago and we had a lovely evening reminiscing. We even took a stroll to look at the house we had all shared in the early 1970's.

When the DVD was completed the children and their parents were invited back for a private viewing in a small theatre. It was very impressive and had certainly been an interesting experience for us all.

The following two years were arguably the happiest of my career. I taught a wonderful class which I took in both Year 5 and Year 6. Twenty girls and ten boys, they were among the nicest children I have ever taught. Highly motivated, although of mixed ability, they produced some of the best Key Stage 2 Sats results the school had ever had. I recall with great fondness, amongst others, Katie, who was an avid and insatiable reader, Siham, who was infatuated with JLS, Monae, a lovely, sparky, talented little girl and Sultan, who was always a true gentleman and a delight to teach.

In many ways I should, perhaps, have called it a day when the class left (on a high note) for their high schools, but I continued for one more year since there were at that time no staff with experience of teaching Year 6 children. I struggled through that final year with a fairly unresponsive group of children and found myself eagerly looking forward to the end of the summer term.

Of course, finally achieving the status of an outstanding teacher in an outstanding school was heart-warming, but I found myself becoming more and more distanced from the children. At my age I had no interest in many of the things which ruled their lives - pop stars, films, reality TV, Facebook etc. I can't imagine what it might be like for today's young teachers when they have to work into their late 60s before they can claim a pension!

Eventually my departure date drew closer. What to do? How to celebrate? It was Amy Boote's idea to hold a 'Tea at the Ritz' themed afternoon. Amy, who worked in the school office, was always full of good ideas. One of my guests, on receipt of the invitation, said, 'How lovely. I've always wanted to go to the Ritz'. I hope she wasn't too crushed when I explained that it was going to be held in the school hall with vintage china, champagne, a string quintet, delicate little sandwiches and dainty cup cakes.

Unfortunately, although it was July, the weather was dreadful and it rained all day. I'd hoped to hold the event in marquees outside in the school grounds, but it wasn't to be. Wayne, our caretaker, was wonderful and erected the marquees in the school hall, later helping to assemble tables and chairs and generally making himself indispensable. He even managed to project beautiful garden scenes with vibrant flowers and cheeping birds onto the large computer screen at the front of the hall.

Amy was a godsend, lifting the whole occasion from the ordinary to the extraordinary. Her finesse in knowing exactly where and how everything should be placed was phenomenal. I told her that she and Wayne should give up their day jobs and become party planners.

Soon enough the ladies arrived wearing their hats and the gentlemen were in lounge suits, at my suggestion. Many of my colleagues from years past had travelled considerable distances to be there and I was both delighted and touched. The present staff sang a song for me and Ann Stringer composed a poem using information about my early life given in secret phone calls by my brother. Both Matt and John gave speeches which were too embarrassing to recall here. It was a bit like being alive at your own funeral, I remember thinking at the time. I tried to lighten proceedings by giving a few humorous anecdotes which went down well, I think.

The champagne slid down easily, the music played by a group of talented young musicians set the background to a delightful atmosphere. I enjoyed it immensely and all too soon the afternoon came to an end.

The following Friday was the last day of term, my last day of teaching and the traditional leavers' assembly, where we say goodbye to our Year 6 and present certificates for merit in a range of fields. As a leaver myself, I said a few words to the assembled Key Stage 2 children which, I hope, led them to believe how happy I had been as a teacher at their school for more than 36 years.

And I had been happy. Otherwise why would I have stayed so long? The staff of the school had always been what had made it all worthwhile. A harmonious, friendly group of people throughout - changes of staff over the years had never changed the ethos and values, the fun and the excitement, the challenges and the fulfilment.

It had been a great career. I wasn't sad to leave. I was ready to embark on the third age of my life. I wouldn't regret it and I wouldn't miss it. As I walked off the premises for the last time I didn't look back, only forward, to what the next stage of my life had to offer.

ND - #0507 - 270225 - C0 - 203/127/13 - PB - 9781861512208 - Matt Lamination